COLLECTED WORK

BERNARD LONERGAN

VOLUME 25

ARCHIVAL MATERIAL:

EARLY PAPERS ON HISTORY

COLLECTED WORKS
OF BERNARD
LONERGAN

ARCHIVAL MATERIAL:
EARLY PAPERS ON
HISTORY

edited by
Robert M. Doran and
John D. Dadosky

Published for Lonergan Research Institute
of Regis College, Toronto
by University of Toronto Press
Toronto Buffalo London

ISBN 978-1-4875-0648-3 (cloth)   ISBN 978-1-4875-2438-8 (paper)

∞ Printed on acid-free, 100% post-consumer recycled paper with
vegetable-based inks.

Library and Archives Canada Cataloguing in Publication

Title: Collected works of Bernard Lonergan.
Other titles: Works. 1988
Names: Lonergan, Bernard J.F., author. | Crowe, Frederick E., editor. |
    Doran, Robert M., 1939– editor. | Dadosky, John D., 1966– editor. |
    Lonergan Research Institute, issuing body.
Description: Includes bibliographical references and indexes. | Contents: v. 25.
    Archival material: early papers on history. | Includes text in English and Latin.
Identifiers: Canadiana (print) 880933283 | ISBN 9781487506483 (v. 25; cloth) |
    ISBN 9781487524388 (v. 25; paper)
Subjects: LCSH: Catholic Church – Doctrines. | LCSH: Philosophy. | LCSH:
    Theology. | LCSH: Education – Philosophy.
Classification: LCC BX891.L595 1988 | DDC 191 – dc20

The Lonergan Research Institute gratefully acknowledges the generous
contribution of The Malliner Charitable Foundation, which has made
possible the production of the entire series.

University of Toronto Press acknowledges the financial assistance to its
publishing program of the Canada Council for the Arts and the Ontario
Arts Council, an agency of the Government of Ontario.

Canada Council   Conseil des Arts
for the Arts   du Canada

ONTARIO ARTS COUNCIL
CONSEIL DES ARTS DE L'ONTARIO
an Ontario government agency
un organisme du gouvernement de l'Ontario

Funded by the   Financé par le
Government   gouvernement
of Canada   du Canada

Canadä

MIX
Paper from
responsible sources
FSC   FSC® C016245
www.fsc.org

Contents

General Editors' Preface, ROBERT M. DORAN / xi

General Editors' Preface

This final volume in Collected Works of Bernard Lonergan consists of eight papers written by Lonergan between 1933 and 1938, all on the topic of history.[1]

After Lonergan's death in November 1984, John Hochban SJ made a preliminary catalogue of a number of his papers, including those he left in his room at Boston College when he moved to the Campion Center in Weston, MA, in March of 1983. These papers were collected into boxes on Lonergan's return to Canada in November of that year. A file marked '713 – History' turned up in 'Box 4.' Hochban recognized its contents immediately as of great importance. While they included more than the eight papers included here, these were both the most original and the most important items in the file.

Michael Shute, a doctoral candidate at Regis College at the time, worked on the eight papers for his dissertation. Michael's work was eventually published: *The Origins of Lonergan's Notion of the Dialectic of History: A Study of Lonergan's Early Writings on History* (Lanham, MD: University Press of America, 1993). Shute divides the eight into two roughly defined 'batches' of four papers each. The editors follow his division and ordering in offering the papers here and rely on his interpretation of each item. His book may now be found under 'Scholarly Works/ Books' on the

---

1 The editors recommend for background information on these papers 'Letter of Bernard Lonergan to the Reverend Henry Keane, S.J.,' *METHOD: Journal of Lonergan Studies* New Series 5:2 (Fall 2014) 23–40.

website www.lonerganresource.com. See chapter 2 for Shute's thinking on the order and dating of the manuscripts, and subsequent chapters for his comments on each one. In the editorial footnotes Shute's book is referred to as *Origins*, with the page numbers being those that appear in the website rendition, not in the printed book.

Numerous relatively short Latin and Greek phrases are translated in the glossary of Latin and Greek words and phrases. The translation of a few longer items is given in footnotes.

No doubt the question will arise as to why this volume is limited to these papers. If we did not have a website devoted to presenting the data contained in Lonergan's archives, this volume would be much longer. But the site www.bernardlonergan.com contains the papers left by Lonergan that are important for the study of his work, including the autograph manuscripts of these essays on history. Critical editing of many of the other papers can and will continue to go forward, and the results will be uploaded to the website. The present papers have been selected for publication in the Collected Works because they disclose the origins of Lonergan's notion of history, summarized in the expression 'progress, decline, and redemption.' Lonergan himself singled out these papers when discussing the origins of *Insight*.[2] That alone is sufficient reason for giving them special status among the items contained in his personal papers.

The major editorial conventions followed here are familiar to the readers of the Collected Works: a general but not slavish reliance on the *Oxford American Dictionary* and the *Chicago Manual of Style*. The original manuscripts do not have any footnotes, and so all footnotes are editorial.

Once again, I thank John Dadosky for joining me in editing this volume, as he did with the second and third *Collections* and *Method in Theology*.

ROBERT M. DORAN
Marquette University

---

2 See Bernard Lonergan, '*Insight* Revisited,' in *A Second Collection*, vol. 13 in Collected Works of Bernard Lonergan, ed. Robert M. Doran and John D. Dadosky (Toronto: University of Toronto Press, 2017) 228–29.

ARCHIVAL MATERIAL:

EARLY PAPERS ON HISTORY

1 Essay in Fundamental Sociology – Philosophy of History[1]

... Listen.

I am all attention, he said.

Unless, said I, either philosophers become kings in our states or those whom we now call our kings and rulers take to the pursuit of philosophy

1 This selection begins with a full page headed 'Essay in Fundamental Sociology,' with the quotation from Plato's *Republic* handwritten in Greek. At the end of the quotation Lonergan references Plato, *Republic*, v, 473d. The remainder of the selection is entitled 'Philosophy of History,' with pagination beginning at 95. Michael Shute proposes the following (*Origins* 68–69):

> That the numbered pages, headed by the title 'Philosophy of History,' begin at 95 and end at 130 indicates that this manuscript is part of a larger work which, as far as we know, no longer exists. It is possible, then, that 'Philosophy of History' is a part of the 'Essay in Fundamental Sociology.' There is some evidence that this might indeed be the case. First, there are references in the manuscript to the quote from Plato which is found in the single sheet with the title 'Essay in Fundamental Sociology' [see below, pp. 14–15]. Second, the description of the contents of an essay Lonergan wrote on the metaphysics of history in his letter to Fr Keane in 1935 indicates a more extensive essay than we now have at hand in 'Philosophy of History.' Third, in ['*Pantōn Anakepalaiōsis*: A Theory of Human Solidarity'] Lonergan makes an explicit connection between the development of a metaphysic of history and the development of a 'Summa Sociologica' [for the latter, see below, p. 57] ... The implication is that Lonergan, at this time, regarded 'metaphysic

seriously and adequately, and there is a conjunction of these two things, political power and philosophical intelligence, while the motley horde of the natures who at present pursue either apart from the other are compulsorily excluded, there can be no cessation of troubles, dear Glaucon, for our states, nor, I fancy, for the human race either. Nor, until this happens, will this constitution which we have been expounding in theory ever be put into practice within the limits of possibility and see the light of the sun. But this is the thing that has made me so long shrink from speaking out, because I saw that it would be a very paradoxical saying. For it is not easy to see that there is no other way of happiness either for private or for public life.

Plato, *Republic*, v, 473 d

———————

of history' and 'summa sociologica' as equivalent terms. In PH ['Philosophy of History'] we find that Lonergan connects his investigations of a philosophy of history to the development of a social philosophy and the use by the Church of a 'scientific sociology.' Thus, the internal and external evidence suggests that there is a reasonable probability that PH was in fact originally a part of the longer 'Essay in Fundamental Sociology.'

To this perhaps there can be added the reference to a 'Summa Philosophica' in the present essay. See below, p. 31.

Shute also maintains (*Origins* 69),

The manuscript of PH is probably the earliest dealing with the dialectic of history, most likely written in 1933–34 during the first two years of Lonergan's studies in theology at the Gregorian University. It is also the longest. In marked contrast to the more concisely formulated arguments of the later documents …, his ideas here are in a stage of initial formulation.

The translation from Plato is by Paul Shorey and appears in *Plato: The Collected Dialogues*, ed. Edith Hamilton and Huntington Cairns (Princeton: Princeton University Press, Bollingen Series lxxi, 1961) 712–13. For Shute's exposition of Lonergan's text, see *Origins* 68–91. Shute has himself provided an earlier edition of this text, in his book *Lonergan's Early Economic Research: Texts and Commentary* (Toronto: University of Toronto Press, 2010) 15–44. The letter to Keane that Shute mentions was published as Bernard Lonergan, 'Letter to Henry Keane, S.J.,' METHOD: *Journal of Lonergan Studies* ns 5:2 (2014, published 2016) 23–40, ed. Frederick E. Crowe and Robert M. Doran. The single page with the quotation from Plato and the entire paper 'Philosophy of History' may be found on www.bernardlonergan.com at, respectively, 71308DOG030 and 71309DTE030.

Philosophy of history [2]

[1 The problem of liberalism] [3]

The significance of the quarrel between church and state is not to be confined to the period extending from the Middle Ages to the successful and complete emergence of liberalism. For however successful liberalism may be considered inasmuch as it holds power, there can be no doubt that this fact of power is at the root of the distempers of the present day. A philosopher cannot be content to ask of history, Who holds the power? He must ask whether this incidence of power is for human progress or for human extinction. There is much in the present world situation to confirm the view that liberalism in power is for the destruction of civilization.

But the philosopher need not confine himself to this single question. To analyze liberalism fundamentally leads to the discovery that there are two aspects to human life: every act of the person is an internal act of will and an external activity; the internal act of the will has been the concern of the church and its opposition to liberalism; the external activity, merely as an external activity, is a motion for an end in its own order, and it has been the control over this order that the liberal states have been vindicating as their right.

[2 Philosophical foundations] [4]

Plainly, we put the question in its full philosophic generality when we ask, What is the end of external human action as such? For if there is an end to individual external acts, and to sets of such external acts, so there must be an end common to all external acts. If we determine this end and determine the laws by which it is attained and under which action to the end evolves, we arrive at what is called a philosophy of history.

---

2 As Shute notes, the work is not subdivided by Lonergan. The editors are following Shute's suggested 'practical division of the material' (Shute, *Origins* 69). Crossed out at the very top, to the right of the title, are the following handwritten words: 'By "liberalism" is to be understood the effective negation of the control of reason as right reason.'
3 See Shute, *Origins* 70–71.
4 See ibid. 71–78.

We define the philosophy of history as the pure theory of external human action. We premise that human action is in its material cause a flow of change – sensible in consciousness, physical in the subconscious and the external world – that it is in its formal cause the emergence of intellectual forms with respect to this flow of change, that it is in its effective control the act of free will, which in itself is an act of love for the intelligible form (*appetitus rationalis sequens formam intellectus*), which in its implicit effect is an approbation or an inhibition of what is happening in the flow of physico-sensitive change. Thus, in the action of the individual there are three things: the physico-sensitive flow of change; the intellectual forms with respect to the phantasmal flux; the power of imposing the intellectual forms upon the flow of change, thus transforming behavior into rational conduct and speech into rational discourse. These three causes merge to constitute a single action: for what is caused by a material, a formal, and an efficient cause is one and not three. Further, it is to be noticed that the basis of the one human flow of action lies in the material-physical-sensible order; what takes place in this order is premoved and (prescinding from the immanent control) predetermined by what takes place outside the individual; on the other hand, the immanent control of intellect and will is no more than a control; it is not a power of initiation but only a power of approval or inhibition. What you can think about depends upon external experience. What you think about it depends upon the mentality you have imbibed from an environment of home, school, university, and the general influences of others. The man with original thoughts from the viewpoint of history is merely an exception to the general rule; he is an instrument of social change, and he is taken into account only in the theory of change and not in the theory of the regular event. Finally, the end of the individual as an individual is to accept the intellectual forms (effective assent to the true, consent to the good); by this means he attains the *energeia*[5] of his personality; on the other hand, inasmuch as he fails to accept the intelligible dictate and make it effective, he is merely predetermined by the physical flow; also, he sins, for sin is

---

5 Of the possible translations given in the lexicon for *energeia*, 'actuation' seems best here. For confirmation, see below, in the next entry, p. 40: 'we find this intelligible individuation [personality] in the actuation of intellect and will in human operation'; and in the third entry, p. 70: 'The act of will as an immanent act is the actuation of a personality, i.e., of an individuation that is independent of matter.'

the failure to obey reason. But on top of this immanent end of individuals there is the external flow of action, which is reasonable or unreasonable according to the goodness of the individuals, which nonetheless is something in itself.

Now we must grasp the intimate connection between the internal and immanent action of man and his external and transient action. This connection is the intelligible unity and the material distinctness of men.

Men are one in possessing one nature. A nature is the intelligible form explaining why a thing is of the kind it is.

Men are many by matter. I am I and not somebody else, not for any assignable or conceivable reason but purely and simply as a matter of fact. Matter is the sensible antecedent to thought in its irreducible form; it is what can never be abstracted from phantasm and so never can be explained; and it can never be abstracted and never explained because there is no explanation, because it is pure matter of fact, the ultimate empirical.

Finally, men are one in their action. *Quidquid movetur ab alio movetur.*[6] This is easily demonstrated. For if anything changed without reference to something else, then it would be from every point of view the sole sufficient reason of its change. If it were the sole sufficient reason of its change, then there would be no change now, but the thing would always have been what it now is becoming. This is a contradiction in terms. To deny the principle of the extrinsic mover is to suppose that a sufficient reason for change is not sufficient for the change at any time and, besides, that it was not sufficient but became sufficient without any sufficient reason for the becoming.

Hence, everything that a man does or thinks is premoved by the action of other things. Further, this premotion extends into the intellectual field and constitutes the premotion of the will. In response to this release of premotion the will need not act: but if it does act, then it acts according to the predetermined intellectual form; if it does not act, then it sins in failing to follow the dictate of reason, while what takes place in action is predetermined by the sensitive mobiles, the previous intellectual pattern, habits, etc., all of which are predetermined.

Thus, besides the unity of human nature there is the unity of human action. Human action is always predetermined to either of two alternatives:

6 Thomas Aquinas, *Summa theologiae*, 1, q. 2, a. 3.

one rational, the other irrational. Which is elected is not ultimately predetermined, though it may be proximately by the person's character or habit of will. Nonetheless, these human elections, though free, are strictly subordinate to a statistical law. Men turn out in ever much the same proportion of good, indifferent, and bad. What differentiates one social epoch from another does not lie in the individual wills of the time but in the upper and lower limits set these wills by the previous age. No man can be better than he knows how, and no man can be worse than his temptations and opportunities. Thus, the heritage of intellectual vacuity and social chaos given by the nineteenth century to the twentieth is the real reason why the twentieth is such a mess.

Now, considering that all that takes place outside the human order in this world is predetermined, considering that all of human action follows the premotions of the material world and previous human action according to a statistical law, we arrive at the conception of history as the flow of human acts proceeding from one human nature, materially individuated in space-time, and all united according to the principle of premotion.

Hence, nature explains why man is of the kind of being that he is.

History explains why men are doing what they are doing.

Matter is the principle which makes the one human nature into a successive manifold of individuals operating the earlier upon the later according to the law of a predetermined bracket of influence and a statistical uniformity within that bracket.

Now, plainly it is impossible to influence human wills to do good without exerting an influence upon the external action that premoves and statistically predetermines wills. This is the claim of the church, of spiritual authority. On the other hand, the flow of human action considered merely as an external flow is for definite ends yet entirely under the control of the wills. This is the basis of the continuous rebellions of the state from medieval times to the present day.

We put the problem on its true philosophic basis by asking the meaning of history, the purpose of the external flow as such.

Now, despite the cries of obscurantists to the contrary, there is as a matter of fact such a thing as progress. It is further manifest that progress is the fundamental concept in any theory of the external flow, the effective solidarity of mankind. For what is important in any flow is its differential. What flowed in the dim and distant past is of no earthly interest to us. But the differentials of what has flowed since integrate into the reality of the present, and that is of supreme concern to us. Further, the differentials of flow are something beyond the elements, the individuals in the flow. The nineteenth century was a century prating of Truth, Beauty, and Goodness. It had no concern for the differentials of flow in virtue of an asinine confidence in political economists. It has landed the twentieth century in an earthly hell. All the good intentions in the world are compatible with all the blunders conceivable. The nineteenth century was a century of good wills and bad intellects. The combination is fatal. Men being reasonable according to their individual lights of reason offer no guarantee that they are reasonable. Nor is any effort of the epoch to stabilize intellect, to make all think alike whether by newspapers, government education, official prejudices and histories[,] and all the rest, any guarantee that the total and the differential of the total wisdom of the epoch is truly intelligent and reasonable. What is needed is a metaphysic of history, a differential calculus of progress.

But what is progress?

It is a matter of intellect. Intellect is understanding of sensible data. It is the guiding form, statistically effective, of human action transforming the sensible data of life. Finally, it is a fresh intellectual synthesis understanding the new situation created by the old intellectual form and providing a statistically effective form for the next cycle of human action that will bring forth in reality the incompleteness of the later act of intellect by setting it new problems.

This follows from the very nature of the human intellect. It is a potency. A potency does not leap to its perfect act but goes through a series of incomplete acts on its way to attaining the perfect act, which is, as St Thomas says, perfect science.[7] Let us generalize. The angelic intellect is instantaneous. It understands all that is to be understood in its individual world simply by being that individuality; it is intellect in act. The human intellect is intellect in potency; it is gradual; it arrives at its perfect act through a series of interactions between objective situations giving rise to intellectual theories and intellectual theories changing objective situations. Finally, as the angelic intellect knows all its to-be-known in the single instant of its being (*aevum*), so the human intellect works through its stages of development in the instant of its being which is all time. Thus, intellectual achievement is not the achievement of individual men, for individual men are unintelligibly different; intellectual achievement is the

7 Ibid., q. 85, a. 3 c.

achievement of the race, of the unity of human action; the individual genius is but the instrument of the race in its expansion.

However, there is such a thing as sound philosophy, that is, definitive knowledge with an immutable basis. Philosophy stands above the shifting scene of time. Its basis is in the pure forms of knowledge. Sense knowledge, even in the perfect act of intellect, will be knowledge of an inexplicable multiplicity: that is, the difference of this point from that, and of this instant from that, and of this particular thing from that, with no possibility of there being any conceivable reason why each point, each instant, each particular thing is the particular that it is and not another. This gives the first element in metaphysical reality: the category of matter. Next, consciousness will always necessarily be a consciousness of action, of something acting, of the self acting: this existing substantial action, this *ens per se*, is no more to be understood in itself as an existing *ens per se* than the difference between points can be explained in terms of more points. We are forced to set up another metaphysical category, which is the ultimate basis of there being anything to be conscious of, just as matter is the ultimate basis of there being anything to perceive; this category is contingence, and contingence can no more be explained in terms of other contingent beings than matter can be explained in terms of more matter; contingence is the ultimate empirical in the order of consciousness just as matter is the ultimate empirical in the order of sense. Finally, there is intellect, and it has its form. This form is the truth of the intelligible. Whenever you understand, you go on to ask whether your understanding is true, for instance, whether the circle really is all that it is because it is the locus of points equidistant from a center. And when you understand that it is, then you know truth. Now truth is true not in virtue of your knowing it. It is true in itself, and the change merely happens in you in virtue of the contingence of your being. Thus, truth as an absolute, as something that is what it is in itself despite what you may happen to think and indifferent to what you happen to think, is the ultimate form of intellect. Perfect science will be true.

Naturally, I can only outline the basis of the immutability of philosophy, of the way it takes hold of elements that will necessarily be found in the ultimate and perfect science of the perfect act of the human intellect. How philosophy sets up a theory of life on the basis of the triple metaphysical category of matter, contingence, and intelligible truth is a question for a different essay much more elaborate than this one. The only point to be made clear at present is the possibility of philosophy, of a universal science that is the form of all science because it rests on the forms, the outer edges, the frames, of all possible human knowledge.

[3 The phases of history][8]

Now the possibility of philosophy leads us to distinguish between two phases in human progress: the automatic stage, in which there is a constant succession of brilliant flowerings and ultimate failures; the philosophic stage, in which the historical expansion of humanity has its ultimate control in a sound philosophy that not only is sound but also is able to guide the expansion effectively.

Next, the actual course of human events divides this division once more into two sections. Hence we have:

(A) The world prior to the discovery of philosophy, that is, up to Socrates, Plato, and Aristotle.
(B) The failure of philosophy to fulfil its social mission, that is, from Plato to the Dark Age.
(C) The automatic cultural expansion following upon the Dark Age and continuing up to the present. It has had sound philosophy but not social consciousness of the social necessity of philosophy.
(D) The future.

We may say a few words of each in turn.

(A) [The world prior to the discovery of philosophy]

This period as a period is either prehistory or revealed truth. Since Catholics believe the Old Testament because they believe the New, we are following a logical order in postponing a consideration of revelation till the emergence of the New Covenant, the Mystery of Faith in the Blood of Christ. Hence we must turn to the prehistorians, and I consider[9] myself fortunate to be able to draw upon Mr Christopher Dawson's undoubtedly brilliant and, by the competent, highly praised *Age of the Gods*.[10]

---

8 See Shute, *Origins* 78–84.
9 The typescript has 'continue.' The change to 'consider' is editorial.
10 Christopher Dawson, *The Age of the Gods: A Study in the Origins of Culture in Prehistoric Europe and the Ancient East* (London and New York: Sheed & Ward, 1933). The book was originally published in 1928, and Lonergan indicates elsewhere that he read it in 1930 or 1931. See *Caring about Meaning: Patterns in the Life of Bernard Lonergan*, ed. Pierrot Lambert, Charlotte Tansey, and Cathleen Going (Montreal: Thomas More Institute Papers, 1982) 9: 'When I was teaching in Regency at Loyola, about

Unfortunately, my memory must act as intermediary between that book and this essay, so I should in advance beg pardon for any inaccuracies.

Let us distinguish the primitive cultures of hunters, fruit-gatherers, fishers, megalith devotees, etc., together with the merely peasant culture marked by painted pottery, from the higher culture of the Mesopotamian Temple States and the Egyptian Dynasties.

The theory of these last two is that the discovery of the ox and large-scale agriculture with its long-term investments necessitated a new idea of property – land that was not merely inviolable as hunting ground but not even to be walked on at will. This idea was made socially effective by the cult of the Mother Goddess, who owned all the land and all its fruits, whose servants the agriculturalists were, from whom each received the bounteous reward of his labors.

We must here notice first of all that the effect of a new means of exploiting matter leads to a greater and more strictly enforced social solidarity. Second, that what differentiates the higher culture of the Near East from the painted-pottery culture generally is this stricter social bond.

For it was in virtue of the socialistic theocracy that the Temple States acquired their capital, supported an expansion of agriculture into its subsidiary arts and crafts, led to richer religious rites with their initial literature of song and their initial science of calendars, formed the basis of a wider expansion through commerce, ultimately to culminate in the stupendous temples such as that of Carchemish and in a caste of priests, the lawgivers, the administrators of justice, the directors of it all.

Next to be noted is that the unity of the Nile valley quickly imposed a political unity or unities, while the Temple States would long continue to flourish as distinct units. But this geographical difference in no way affected the ultimate result. The god or goddess that is tied down and sacred to only one spot is unequal to the task of imposing social order beyond his frontier. The gods of the states made commercial treaties to quarrel again till finally the whole was swallowed up in a Babylon. Priests yielded to warrior kings.

1930–31, I read *The Age of the Gods*.' From the next sentence in the present text, we gather that Lonergan was not able to find the book in Rome. *The Age of the Gods* was reissued by the Catholic University of America Press in 2012.

Finally must be observed the nature of empire, of bureaucratic rule. It is vigorous as long as it continues to expand, for then it has a social purpose to which all else is subordinate. But expansion inevitably yields to space; decreasing returns are as much a phenomenon of empire as of business. Next, once the expansion is ended, there is no social purpose beyond preserving what has been achieved. A bureaucracy cannot integrate the individual differential forces that would make for change and advancement; it suppresses them; it rules by rule of thumb which, however excellent at the beginning of the rule, becomes more and more antiquated, more and more the understanding of a situation that is anything but the existing situation. Hence, when there is no tendency to advance, a bureaucracy merely encases a mummy, though the mummies of Egypt have lasted longer than her dynasties. On the other hand, given a fundamentally new idea, the bureaucracy passes away in a bath of blood.

But, though the ancient empires could not produce such an idea as could the liberals in the French Revolution and the Bolsheviks in Russia, the human spirit was not eternally baulked. The empires of Egypt, Babylon, Crete, Assyria, the Hittites passed away, and on their ruins, though on the fringe of their frontiers, were born the city states of Greece. Here we have the same phenomenon as the Temple States, the small social unit that is not primarily a unit of blood but of geographical position. But there is the difference that the Greeks did not owe their rise to sages who called themselves priests but to sages who were simply lawgivers, the leaders of comrades who fought side by side in battle. Death, the great leveler, is at the root of democracy. And democracy was the social form that made philosophy possible.

Gotama would have been as great a dialectician as Socrates had he lived in Athens. But he lived where men had not the habit of demanding the reason why for everything, of listening to orators and appraising their arguments, of following the sophists to learn to be orators themselves. This social fact differentiated Socrates from all the wise and profound men who preceded him. It was the birth of philosophy, of following reason like a breeze, blow where it will. It was the promise of the eternal search for the reasons for everything up to the *ultimum cur*.

But philosophy had other presuppositions. Not only had to be dispelled the herd instinct of being satisfied with what the wise man said without bothering for any 'why' beyond the fact that he was wise; there was the need of a rich and precise language, of a literature to make men think of man in general terms, of science to reveal there was such a thing as science, and so the possibility of a science of science.

(B) [The failure of philosophy to fulfil its social mission]

Philosophy emerged with the assertion of its social significance. 'Men and cities will not be happy till philosophers are kings' is the central position of Plato's *Republic*, and the *Republic* is the center of the dialogues. To Plato, Pericles, the idol of Athenian aspirations, was an idiot; he built docks and brought the fruits of all lands to Athens and beautified the city and pursued a policy of anticipating enemies while they were still weak; but he neglected the one thing necessary, the true happiness of the citizens. For did not the dialectic reveal that no man without self-contradiction could deny that suffering injustice was better than doing injustice, that pain was compatible with happiness, that shame, the interior contradiction, the lie in the soul of a man to himself, was incompatible with happiness? And whom had Socrates ever met that he could not reduce to nonsense?[11] To put the truth in an easier form, let me recall a sentence from one of Mr Dawson's reflective essays: you can give men better homes and food and clothing; you can build them theatres and parks and recreation grounds; you can decrease their labor and increase their wages and multiply a thousandfold the products of industry and the earth; and still men will not be content: but you can lead them through pain and misery, through toil and privation, and they will be happy if only they have something to die for.[12] The point is a commonplace of history and literature; it is a fundamental element of human psychology; and it is none the less true because the nineteenth-century liberals believed exactly the contrary.

The function, then, of the state is to teach virtue. But to teach virtue you must know it; only the philosopher can know it; none but the philosopher may be king, if the state is to attain its end, if men are to be happy.

11 See the references to the *Gorgias* below, p. 108 and note 23, and p. 171 and note 26. See also p. 86.
12 https://www.brainyquote.com/authors/christopher_dawson: 'You can give men food and leisure and amusements and good conditions of work, and still they will remain unsatisfied. You can deny them all these things, and they will not complain so long as they feel that they have something to die for.' See chapter 5, 'Religion,' in Christopher Dawson, *The Modern Dilemma: The Problem of European Unity* (London and New York: Sheed & Ward, 1932) 97.

We cannot but grant the truth of the Platonic position; its truth is quite a different matter from its practicability. But we must measure both the strength and weakness of Platonism. It was evident to anyone contemplating what made and unmade statesmen in Athens, what determined the policies of the city states, what was the worth of the statesmen, the voters, the policies, what was the inevitable outcome, that there was an imperative need of a higher control. This was as evident to Plato then as it is evident today, whether we cast our eyes within the frontiers of our ever so sovereign states or beyond into the chaos of international diplomacy, or close our eyes to the present, with the relief of waking from a nightmare, to meditate on the rise and decline of all cultures and political forms. They did not pass away because some stronger thing arose to crush them; they passed away because they first decomposed. The march of Alexander through the Near East, like the march of the semi-barbarian legionaries through the Roman Empire, was but the profanation of a corpse and the scattering of the ashes of what long since lay dead. But, however great the need for a higher control, for the rule of reason socially dominant and freeing society from a cyclic karma as the rule of reason frees an individual man from the intermittent domination and ultimate collapse of his passions, what we have to consider was the possibility of Platonism meeting the need.

The achievement of Platonism lay in its power of criticism. The search for a definition of virtue in the earlier dialogues establishes that virtue is an irreducible something, the emergence of a new light upon experience that cannot be brought back and expressed in terms of experience. This discovery of the idea, of intelligible forms, gave not only the dialectic but also the means of social criticism. For it enabled men to express not by a symbol but by a concept the divine.

Primitive men could understand that there was a God, but they could no more express this act of understanding that transcended experience than Einstein can make you a working model of space-time so that you will be able to understand the way he understands physical phenomena. They expressed symbolically this understanding; they tended to vary their symbols with the form of their society; the hunters had mystic animals; the peasants the Mother Goddess and her consort; and the Egyptian cults offer an interesting example of a superposition of the latter on the former; then there were the sky-gods of the nomads familiar in Greek, Roman, and Teutonic mythology, while the cult of the dead, the sacredness of the family tie, the beauties of nature and its terrors provided a subsidiary host.

The supreme difficulty of substituting a concept for symbolism is borne in upon us by the constant warnings of the Hebrew prophets, which had their ground in the constant backslidings of the Hebrew people. The same example shows us the dangers of symbolism, the ease with which it passed into idolatry and superstition and, finally, orgiastic lust, whether in the somber cruelty of Baal or the routs of Dionysus. Nor is the origin of such degradation hard to find. The security and wealth of the settled state, where religion tends to be the symbolism of a concrete utility, social order, provide quite a different psychological setting from the isolation and misery of primitive men; there is quite manifestly a temptation to think of the present good as the meaning of religion in the former case while only the transcendent can be good in the latter. Again, religion is the explanation of reality, and reality offers a twofold aspect: good and evil. This gives rise to a polytheism which even Plato hardly dared oppose. He was content that the gods be good, that men did not seek to justify their passions by painting the gods as worse than such as enjoy a Mohammedan paradise.

As the basis of social reform, Plato criticized the gods and goddesses of Greece, and in this he sought to make education his ally by purifying it of its manifest corruptions. But his positive work was weak. His guardians were trained in what can only be called a school of mysticism, yet mysticism is hardly an art to be acquired even in its natural, merely metapsychic forms. His theory of marital communism was a failure, however excusable in Greece, to grasp the significance in social life of monogamy and the education of children, since parents love their children even as Plato loved his philosophy with a love equally disinterested and far more easily attained. Finally, his crossing out 'mine' and 'thine' from the dictionary was but using a bludgeon where is needed a rapier.

Plato's greatness lies in his fidelity to the social problem in its most acute form. His *Republic*, like Kant's *Kritik*, set a perfect question but utterly failed to answer it. But Plato stayed with his task. He tried to develop the dialectic in a series of dialogues that puzzle the modern student from their mixture of profound and simple problems that are all taken with equal earnestness. He remained a teacher, never putting forth an idea that was not so refined and polished that a smart lad could not get the point from the other end of the dialectical game. But eventually he renounced his projected *Philosophos* and with it philosophy; he wrote the *Laws* in an attempt to play in his very modern times the glorious role of the sage and lawgiver of days so long gone by. He passed his mantle on to Aristotle, but for Aristotle the one issue was science, and the only science of Ethics that Aristotle would attempt was a practical ethics that neatly dodged the real questions about the ultimate of society.

The stream of practical influence that proceeded from Socrates forgot Plato and Aristotle, to divide into Cynic and Cyrenaic, Stoic and Epicurean. The Epicurean simply renounces all attempt at higher control; the Stoic manfully seeks it but can succeed only for the individual, teaching all men, but more popular in times of stress and general misfortune than in times of joy, and, when popular, not teaching men to achieve but only to die with dignity.

The gods and goddesses that Plato mildly rebuked remained as strong as ever, a pall of gibbering ghosts to dim the luster of the decaying empire of Rome. The Stoics, whether the victims of imperial arbitrariness or the rulers from the throne of the Caesars, could not halt that decay. And though in the fourth century Christianity was an ever-growing and manifest power, still Christ had not come to save the world.[13]

(C)   [The automatic cultural expansion following upon the
        Dark Age and continuing up to the present]

This period is a continuous advance accompanied by a continuous retrogression. The initial situation are [*sic*] the infinitesimal unities that were later integrated into the feudal hierarchy and, on the other hand, the Christian Church. From the church canonists came the laws that were the basis of an economic expansion by commerce, just as previously from the monastic centers came the agriculture that was the foundation of commerce. The full flowering of these two may be represented by the gothic

---

13 The meaning of this sentence is perhaps expressed in the following
   sentences written by Lonergan about forty years later: 'Christianity
   developed and spread within the ancient empire of Rome. It possessed the
   spiritual power to heal what was unsound in that imperial domain. But
   it was unaccompanied by its natural complement of creating, for a single
   development has two vectors, one from below upwards, creating, the other
   from above downwards, healing. So when the Roman empire decayed and
   disintegrated, the church indeed lived on. But it lived on, not in a civilized
   world, but in a dark and barbarous age in which, as a contemporary
   reported, men devoured one another as fishes in the sea.' Bernard
   Lonergan, 'Healing and Creating in History,' in *A Third Collection*, vol. 16
   in Collected Works of Bernard Lonergan, ed. Robert M. Doran and John
   D. Dadosky (Toronto: University of Toronto Press, 2017) 102–103.

cathedrals and the monarchies not yet exalted by any absolutist doctrine of the divine right of kings. Again from the church came the universities and the Scholastic science which put Christianity on a far higher natural basis than had been known in the early church. The scandal of the antipopes was the turning point of the whole period. For when in Italy, more under Byzantine influence than under that of the Nordic culture, which may be represented by a circle with its center at Aix-la-Chapelle (C. Dawson),[14] the discovery of ancient literature not only gave a new birth to modern literature but as well cast a glamour over ancient paganism, a section of the North was able to secede from the intellectual unity of Christendom: this secession had a double cause, pagan corruption and the obscuration of papal authority. History now flows in two streams, and the villain of the piece is the state. The state stabilized the heresies. The wars of religion between the states, in which religion was not the determining factor (Richelieu), gave birth to a new principle, Liberalism: this was the negation of the need of higher control; what Plato longed for, the liberal threw away. The liberal state considered itself an absolute sovereign, as much the Catholic as the Protestant, as much the kings as the later democracies. Meanwhile the positive progress continued; to law and Scholastic philosophy and modern literature was added the deliriously brilliant achievement of mathematical science. Science combined with liberalism to make political economy and to transfer power from an aristocracy to a plutocracy. Liberalism is a fact not a theory: but it inevitably tends to either of two theories, modernism or Bolshevism, neither of which are autonomous theories but arise from the objective situation and represent two directions that may be adopted to make it a consistent unity. The modernist desires to leave the whole of history without any higher control: all thought that is not positive science has no justifiable application to the objective situation, since such thought has only a subjective value; all thought that is positive science merely represents inevitable law, the truth of what is going to happen in any case. The Bolshevist on the contrary takes as his starting point precisely the indifference of the modernist to the objective situation, argues that his religion is merely a sham, an opiate to soothe the misery of those oppressed by the modern-

---

14 Lonergan may have in mind Christopher Dawson, *Progress and Religion: An Historical Inquiry* (London: Sheed & Ward, 1929/1931) 178. Lonergan is likely referring to Aix-la-Chapelle (German = Aachen) as the center because it was at one time the unofficial capital of the Holy Roman Empire.

ist state. However, Bolshevism uses theory only as a starting point: its intrinsic nature is the domination of the *fait accompli*. It is the science of propaganda, the strategy of revolution, the political creed of cowing men by brutality and terror, and the art of permanently winning their hearts by moral perversion. As Mme Kollontai[15] put it: 'Immorality is progressing favorably in the schools.' Bolshevism is ludicrous with its initial assertion that man is no more than an animal; but Bolshevism is terrible in its power to prove its own truth by making man no more than an animal.

The present situation is, on the one hand, the Bolshevist assertion of the animal in man and, on the other hand, the church's absolute assertion of the spiritual nature of man. Between these two historic forces lie the liberal sovereign states with their economic problems and their political hatreds and fears: these are the pawns in the game, however solid they may appear with their devotion to whatever is merely because it is.

We now return to the general theory, which we left with the division of progress into automatic and philosophic. We observe that the initial automatic period led automatically to the emergence of philosophy. Intellect discovered the possibility of social organization for the fuller exploitation of material goods; this took the form of a socialistic theocracy and gave rise to all the material achievement of man up to the industrial revolution; it laid the basis for the enrichment of language into literature and the discovery of science; the postulate of higher control over commerce changed the rule of priests into a rule of warriors; on this followed decay because the warriors could do nothing more once they had an empire. Still, out of the ancient culture and on the fringe of its influence arose the no longer nomadic warrior and so the democratic city states of Greece; democracy made philosophy possible.

15 Alexandra Mikhailovna Kollontai (1872–1952), a Russian Communist revolutionary. Lonergan may be recalling an essay by Edmund A. Walsh, 'The Catholic Church in Present-Day Russia,' *The Catholic Historical Review* 18:2 (1932) 197. Walsh writes: 'The atmosphere of crass materialism and positive atheism which envelops the official school system [of Soviet Russia] has released the growing generation from obedience to parents or to conscience. When a state deliberately breaks down the barrier of parental and spiritual authority provided by the home and the church, it is opening a floodgate which no other human power can control. Add to this the influence of Madame Kollontai, with her doctrines of free love, free marriage, and jungle promiscuity, and the demoralizing circle is completed. How corruptive her influence has been may be judged from her novel, *Red Love*. The progress of immorality in the schools is her outstanding achievement. A decent respect for the common opinion of mankind prevents me from quoting the circumstantial portions of her various reports and recommendations.'

Next to be observed is the impotence of philosophy to fulfil its function of higher control. Men want symbols, and philosophy postulates concepts.

Third to be observed is the fact that Christianity was at once a symbol and a trans-philosophic higher control. In consequence, modern history as a progress is in the reverse order to ancient history. The moderns began with philosophy, went on to literature, developed science, and then applied it. The ancients first learnt the practical arts, then literature, then science, and finally philosophy. On the other hand, the Reformation does not differ from polytheism, and liberalism does not differ from the depravation of polytheism: the Reformation accepted the states instead of the church because there was something it did not understand; liberalism denied higher control to bring theory into accordance with objective fact.

Fourth to be observed is that while the ancient cycle was a dialectic of fact, the modern cycle was a dialectic of thought: these differ in that the dialectic of fact has its first motion in material needs (socialistic agriculture, empire, democracy, more empire), [while] the dialectic of thought has its first motion from thought (canon law, monarchy, philosophy from theology, applied science from theoretical science).

Fifth to be observed is that the retrograde movement in the modern period arises from the superposition of the dialectic of fact upon the dialectic of thought. The Reformation appealed to the councils above the antipopes (not really so but apparently so, which is the point of this dialectic); liberalism appealed to the religious wars as fought for nothing (true of the way they were fought but not true of what they might have been fought for); modernism appealed to Kantian agnosticism (a problem not a philosophy); communism appealed to the indifference of religion to the social problem (true of some religion, namely, such as does not vindicate its right to dictate to all consciences as consciences on all issues).

Sixth comes the emergence of the pure dialectic of fact, the realization of the materialist conception of history that Karl Marx supposed to be the true conception of history. Bolshevism deals only with facts: but it makes the facts it deals with.

Seventh, we prove our assertion that the state is the villain of the modern piece.[16] For, insofar as the state really could progress, it had to be

16 Crossed out after 'piece': 'Distinguish from the state the function of internal economic order, the administration of justice and the development of laws with its presupposition of a plan of social progress.'

subject to the higher control of intellect. The higher control of intellect we may honestly attribute neither to the general run of kings nor of parliaments. Yet as long as the state was subject to the higher intellectual control, it was in continuous rebellion; when it laid this control aside (Reformation and Gallicanism),[17] it surrendered itself hands bound to the domination of economic law (liberalism). In both cases, it deliberately fostered the mere dialectic of fact in the form of nationalism – the stupid appeal to a common language and a united geographical position as something of real significance. In both cases, it had to do this: in the former to have a weapon against spiritual authority; in the latter to have a weapon against economic rivals.[18]

(D) [The future]

We turn to the philosophic estimate of the future.

The first point to be noted is that the antinomy of church and state is fundamental. The state is the social expression of the natural ambitions and desires of man; it is the home of literature with its universal outlook from the mysticism of romanticism to the sober, humanistic beauty of classicism and naturally ordered human life; it is the support of scientific effort with its inward enthusiasms and outwardly manifest benefits; it is the common effort of a people whose mentality is molded by a common language, common manners, common historical memories of triumphs and deep grievances, to carry on the work of human advancement till the dream of a democracy which is an aristocracy for all be realized. But not only does the state sum up the natural ambitions and desires of man at their best; it is the real power of modern times as in any time in the past. It deliberately exploits all that is excellent and much that is evil in the social mentality and in the desires of individuals to make its power an absolute and unquestionable power.

17 '(Reformation and Gallicanism)' were inserted by hand as was '(liberalism)' at the end of the sentence.
18 Crossed out here: 'Eighth, we observe that the state had a real problem. There was in the philosophy of the spiritual authority no systematic recognition and official encouragement of progress after the counter reformation.' See below, p. 34, at note 38.

Against this stands the church with its foundation not in the outward flow of history but in the consciences of individuals. For the church to take advantage of state support is, indeed, in the reasonable order of things. But this support is in the last analysis no addition to the church's real foundation, which is in the individual conscience; it is a support that will weather the squalls and the smaller storms of the historical process; it is not a support that will see the church through the incessant drag of the dialectic of fact. For this dialectic also has its hold on the conscience. The good men would do, they do not do. This contradiction in the conscience itself ever tends to the rationalism of making wrong into right. Till wrong is openly asserted to be right, sin is but an incidental element in the historic flow; it is a constant that vanishes when one differentiates to find the forces. But when wrong sets itself up as a theory, then it becomes a force; then sin really enters into the world; then men are unconsciously corrupted. This corruption is not merely moral; it is not merely the generalization and universalization of the defended sin; it is a continuous potentiality of further rationalism, for the false that is in men's minds seeks to be made consistent with the truth that they possess, and the process inevitably ends with the falsification of all that is true. Once error has found an entrance in the name of sin, it can hardly be exorcized. For to crush the error, the sin must first be crushed; and *ex hypothesi* the sin could not be crushed even when men had the truth.

Against the rationalizing dialectic of fact, the church has a double weapon: to remove the contradiction from the individual conscience, to make the sinner affirm that sin is sin and so preclude the possibility of his trying to make out that sin is not sin, there is the sacrament and the practice of auricular confession; to crush any incipient movement of rationalization in the social field, there is the teaching magisterium of the church. Together, these two form a perfect bulwark. Hence the heretics of the sixteenth century had to precede the rationalists of the eighteenth, just as the rationalists of the eighteenth century had to precede the communists of our own. On the other hand, everything in the modern mentality outside the church – insofar as that mentality rests upon tradition set up since the Reformation – is necessarily in opposition to the church. Only the mind that can sweep away the whole of the outlook imposed upon it by its environment is capable of coming back to the church: the difficulty of the task may be estimated by the fact that it took Newman over fifteen years to do so. However highly we estimate the power of the church to attract souls, we must remember that those attracted must from the nature of the case be a select minority. The first three centuries of Christianity gave the conversion of only from ten to twenty percent of the Roman Empire.

Liberalism is the supreme social doctrine of modern times, in Catholic countries as well as non-Catholic. Intrinsically, that is, as far as logic goes, liberalism is simply a cypher: the assertion that logic has nothing to do with the control of social life, with history. It was on this ground that we asserted liberalism to be the pawn between Bolshevism and Catholicism. It may last for centuries, as did Egypt, Babylon, Rome. It cannot last forever. The political mechanism on which it rests is the ability of England to maintain the balance of power on the continent of Europe – a process that will last just so long as no power on the continent can snap its fingers at England. When that day comes, we shall have a European empire; a beneficent despot or an utter tyrant according to circumstance and mood; absolute, for the modern means of warfare give a central government as great a power over a greater area as did gunpowder to the monarchs; great or insignificant, according to the carnage and cost of the initial achievement; decadent, for the economic problem will remain, and a socialistic empire is not a solution.

Meanwhile, we note that the modern state has no claim to be a sovereign state, to make final and absolute decisions. First, because no modern state is a perfect society. A perfect society has the right of making final and absolute decisions because it holds under its control and responsibility all that is affected by the decisions. No modern state, generally speaking, is either economically or politically independent. The world is run by an oligarchy of *Grossmächte*, and the justice of their decisions is as much open to question as the existence of their right to make decisions.

Thus, there is a triple reason for the liquidation of the present order of sovereign states. First, they must be conducted on no intelligible principle; they must argue not from what ought to be but solely from what is; they cannot but be liberal, else they are not sovereign. Second, sound social theory as theory can assign no basis to their pretended right to making absolute decisions; they are neither economically nor politically independent, and therefore they are not sovereign. Third, their action is immoral and cannot but be immoral. It is immoral in the domination of the Great Powers: even were they wise and just, they have not the right to make the decisions that they do make. Further, it is immoral in the fomentation of nationalism by the perversion of the newspaper, the school, and practically everything else: nationalism is the setting up of a tribal god not merely in the case of Germany – at whom the world smiles for its self-idolatry – but in every case; every nation foments nationalism according to its need;

Germany's exaltation of the nation is only the index of a greater need; every country does so, because no country in the present situation can be conducted on an intelligible principle, and so it must be conducted on an asinine principle. Again, the action of the sovereign states is necessarily immoral in the matter of armament manufacture: no country dare tell the private firms to close up shop, because no country knows when it will need them. And not only in this matter but in every economic question the antiquated sovereignty of the state is the fundamental difficulty; this will sufficiently appear from our discussion of economics.[19]

When we pass from liberalism to Bolshevism we descend to a lower level in the dialectic of fact. The liberal argues from what is; the Bolshevist argues from what the Bolshevist by propaganda, revolution, terrorism, and sexual perversion will make of man. As the barbaric legionaries destroyed the decaying Roman Empire, Bolshevism will do all it can to destroy the decaying liberal world. The Bolshevik is not considered a power in the modern world much as Philip of Macedon was not considered a power in the Greek world. It is not impossible that all attempts to unite Europe will be as futile as Demosthenes' Philippics. But it is manifest that the modern Philip has a hold upon the modern states not only in his power of arms but also in his power to win the allegiance of everyone in the liberal states who wishes justice but not Christ.

[4 The dialectical division of history][20]

Before attempting the synthesis, we distinguish:

The absolute dialectic: revelation, prophecy, development of dogma.

The dialectic of fact:

(a) Mere fact: the ancient higher culture of the Near East.
(b) Sin: the corruption of ancient culture and the beginning of the corruption of modern culture.
(c) Revealed fact: the development of the Jews and of Christendom up to the end of the Middle Ages.

19 See below, p. 32, at note 37, for a possible indication of what is meant by 'our discussion of economics.'
20 See Shute, *Options* 84–86.

The dialectic of thought:

(a) Natural reason: Plato's attempt at a social philosophy.
(b) Rationalism: Reformation, liberalism, Bolshevism.
(c) Faith: Scholastic social theory culminating in the encyclicals of His Holiness, Pius XI.[21]

[5 The necessity of the supernatural][22]

We observe an anomaly, the necessity of the supernatural and the fact that the supernatural does not eliminate a dialectic based upon sin as a datum for irreflective action or for theory of what is, even though sin is *non-ens*. The necessity of the supernatural appears in the failure of the ancients to produce a social philosophy and the fact that the modern secular dialectic of thought made sin a datum for its social theory to end with the cult of sin, Bolshevism. The fact that the supernatural does not eliminate a dialectic based on sin appears both in the ultimate corruption of the Jews who crucified Christ (irreflective dialectic of sin) and in the scandal of the antipopes, the Reformation, and the subsequent dialectic of thought that had sin for its premise. We note in passing that the hope of the future lies in a philosophic presentation of the supernatural concept of social order: it must be guided by the faith, for reason alone is inadequate, as we see both in the failure of Plato's thought and in the impossibility of presenting pure philosophy as an *idée-force*; but though supernatural it must also be philosophic, for only a sound philosophy can establish the intellectual conviction necessary to reassure men, can eliminate false theories in a purely natural sphere, can give positive guidance in what the Pope called in his encyclical 'technical matters' lying outside the scope of his pastoral office.[23]

It will be useful to ask in what this necessity of the supernatural, as revealed by the dialectic, consists.

It is a necessity not of nature but of action.

21 Lonergan is referring in particular to 'Quadrigesimo Anno.' See http://w2 .vatican.va/content/pius-xi/en/encyclicals/documents/hf_p-xi_enc_19310515 _quadragesimo-anno.html. See § 88. See also below, p. 58, note 32.
22 See Shute, *Options* 86–87.
23 See 'Quadrigesimo Anno' § 41.

Human action is one: a statistically predetermined flow; all the individual can do is accept or reject the intellectual forms supplied him for the guidance of his action by the environment; if he thinks of anything not supplied him by the environment, he is merely incidental, or he is an instrument used by humanity to bring forth a new idea which will become part of some existing movement or the initiation of a new movement.

The necessity of the supernatural for action does not prove that the supernatural is not supernatural. The supernatural is what transcends nature in its constituents, consequents, exigences. The need of the supernatural for action does not contradict this transcendence of nature. For the need of the supernatural for action has its sole premise in sin. But sin is not a constituent of nature; it is not a consequence of nature; nor does nature by sinning establish any exigence in the order of rights but only a petition to the Divine Mercy for the gratuitousness of grace.

But it would seem that sin establishes an exigence in the order of rights: the present generation suffers for the sins of the past; that the present should suffer for the past is unjust.

That the present should suffer for the past is not unjust, for humanity is not an aggregation of individuals. It is one reality in the order of the intelligible. It is a many in virtue of matter alone. Now any right and any exigence has its foundation only in the intelligible. Matter is not the basis of exigence but the basis of potentiality. *The one intelligible reality, man, humanity, unfolds by means of matter into a material multiplicity of men, that the material multiplicity may rise, not from itself, but from the intelligible unity, to an intelligible multiplicity of personalities.*[24] Men become from man as grapes from the one vine; if the vine corrupts, so do the grapes; but the grapes suffer no injustice from the vine; they are but part of the vine.

[6 The supernatural component of the dialectic][25]

As is plain, there is a peculiar relation between the earlier and the later in history. We put this relation in the limiting case when we think of the first man. For the first man sinned, leaving man *spoliatus gratuitis, vulneratus in naturalibus.*[26] *Spoliatus gratuitis,* for the unity of human nature lost its

24 What is here italicized is presented in upper-case letters in Lonergan's typescript.
25 See Shute, *Options* 87–89.
26 Thomas Aquinas, *Super II Sententiarum,* d. 29, q. 1, a. 2.

divine adoption. *Vulneratus in naturalibus*, for the course of history was reversed: man, instead of developing from an initial knowledge of philosophy, had to develop by the exploitation of matter in a social form. In addition to this was set up the awful tradition of sin. '... by one man sin entered into this world and by sin death; and so death passed upon all men, in whom all have sinned' (Romans 5.12).[27] But there was a second Adam, to restore the divine adoption by a new creation, to set up as first mover a new tradition of grace. 'For if by the offense of *one*, *many* died: much more the grace of God and the gift, by the grace of *one* man, Jesus Christ, hath abounded unto *many*. And not as it was by *one* sin, so also is the gift. For judgment indeed was by *one* unto condemnation: but grace is of *many* offenses unto justification. For if by *one* man's offense death reigned through *one*: much more they who receive abundance of grace and of the gift and of justice shall reign in life through *one*, Jesus Christ. Therefore, as by the offense of *one*, unto *all* men to condemnation: so also by the justice of *one*, unto *all* men to justification of life. For as by the disobedience of *one* man, *many* were made sinners: so also by the obedience of *one*, *many* shall be made just' (Romans 5.15–19).[28] There is no need to argue that we have here an insistence upon the metaphysical and physical relations of the one and the many: the metaphysical in Adam's loss of grace and Christ's restoration of it in a 'new creation'; the physical in the fact that sin set up the dialectic of fact to bring about the 'many offenses' and the general corruption of history. 'For we have charged both Jews and Greeks that they are all under sin. As it is written: There is not any man just. There is none that understandeth: there is none that seeketh after God. All have turned out of the way: they are become unprofitable together: there is none that doth good, there is not so much as one. Their throat is an open sepulchre: with their tongues they have dealt deceitfully. The venom of asps is under their lips. Whose mouth is full of cursing

---

27 NRSV: 'sin came into the world through one man, and death came through sin, and so death spread to all because all have sinned.'

28 Emphasis is Lonergan's. NRSV: 'For if the many died through the one man's trespass, much more surely have the grace of God and the free gift in the grace of the one man, Jesus Christ, abounded for the many. And the free gift is not like the effect of the one man's sin. For the judgment following one trespass brought condemnation, but the free gift following many trespasses brings justification. If, because of the one man's trespass, death exercised dominion through that one, much more surely will those who receive the abundance of grace and the free gift of righteousness exercise dominion in life through the one man, Jesus Christ.'

and bitterness: their feet swift to shed blood: destruction and misery in their ways: and the way of peace they have not known. There is no fear of God before their eyes' (Romans 3.9–18). [29] 'And as they liked not to have God in their knowledge, God delivered them up to a reprobate sense, to do those things which are not convenient. Being filled with all iniquity, malice, fornication, avarice, wickedness: full of envy, murder, contention, deceit, malignity: whisperers, detractors, hateful to God, contumelious, proud, haughty, inventors of evil things, disobedient to parents, foolish, dissolute: without affection, without fidelity, without mercy. Who, having known the justice of God, did not understand that they who do such things are worthy of death: and not only they that do them, but they also that consent to them that do them' (Romans 1.28–32). [30] These are the many offenses, the height of human corruption, arising from the refusal to have God in human knowledge, and brought about by a corporate responsibility of those who do evil and those that consent to evildoers. Now Christ not only restores the divine adoption: he is also the first mover of a new order. But 'not as it was by one sin, so also is the gift.' The one sin proceeds from its unity to the many offenses; but the gift proceeds from the many offenses unto one justification in Christ Jesus. The many offenses are brought under a higher control, are integrated into a new movement, 'in the dispensation of the fullness of times, to re-establish

29 NRSV: '... for we have already charged that all, both Jews and Greeks, are under the power of sin, as it is written: "There is no one who is righteous, not even one; there is no one who has understanding, there is no one who seeks God. All have turned aside, together they have become worthless; there is no one who shows kindness, there is not even one. Their throats are opened graves; they use their tongues to deceive. The venom of vipers is under their lips. Their mouths are full of cursing and bitterness. Their feet are swift to shed blood; ruin and misery in their paths, and the way of peace they have not known. There is no fear of God before their eyes."'

30 NRSV: 'And since they did not see fit to acknowledge God, God gave them up to a debased mind and to things that should not be done. They were filled with every kind of wickedness, evil, covetousness, malice. Full of envy, murder, strife, deceit, craftiness, they are gossips, slanderers, God-haters, insolent, haughty, boastful, inventors of evil, rebellious toward parents, foolish, faithless, heartless, ruthless. They know God's decree, that those who practice such things deserve to die – yet they not only do them but even applaud others who practice them.'

(*anakephalaiōsai*, integrate) all things in Christ, that are in heaven and on earth, in him' (Ephesians 1.10).[31]

Let us study this movement of integration, of bringing the scattered elements of humanity, no longer submissive to the law of reason, back under the control of that law.

There is no difficulty in identifying the unity of human action that is consequent to the action of Christ as a new prime mover in society, a second Adam, with what is called the mystical body of Christ, that is, the 'many' of his metaphysical 'one' in the 'new creation' of humanity. In this new creation there are the two aspects of nature and action: nature is elevated by sanctifying grace; action is made good by actual grace. As we deal with the theory of human action, we concentrate attention on the latter.

I would define actual grace as the premotion consequent to Christ. Its social form is the *koinōnia*, the sharing with Christ, the communion with Christ. In itself, this social form has a fourfold aspect. As a body that lives by the blood of Christ, it is the eternal priesthood according to the order of Melchisedech and the sacraments that apply the grace of Christ's sacrifice. As a body that is but an extension of the body of Christ, it exercises a power of jurisdiction, admitting members into the body by baptism, excluding decayed cells from the organism by excommunication. As a body united to Christ as Head, it is of one mind and with the authority of a divinely constituted teacher; 'we have the mind of Christ' (1 Corinthians 2.16), and that mind is not only one but authoritative. Finally, as Christ's Body, it executes the will of the Head, of him who exclaimed: 'Jerusalem, Jerusalem, thou that killest the prophets and stonest them that are sent unto thee, how often would I have gathered together thy children, as the hen doth gather her chickens under her wings, and thou wouldst not!' [Matthew 23.37].[32] It is in the body of Christ that the Christian lives and moves, lives the life of a soul elevated to the supernatural order, moves in obedience to the *idée-force*; the intelligible or rather transintelligible form which by revelation is the Christian's dictate of reason. Christ is the vine, and we are the branches. By him we are all that we are, for being is act

---

31 NRSV: 'as a plan for the fullness of time, to gather up all things in him, things in heaven and things on earth.' Note Lonergan's suggested translation for *anakephalaiōsai*: 'integrate.' See below, p. 39, note 3.

32 NRSV: 'Jerusalem, Jerusalem, the city that kills the prophets and stones those who are sent to it! How often have I desired to gather your children together as a hen gathers her brood under her wings, and you were not willing!'

and every act has its premotion, while sin is non-act, *non-ens*, the failure of the will to perform its immanent act of love for the intelligible form which makes action rational.

But the Christian and the social form of Christianity, the church, is in the world. 'I pray not that thou shouldst take them out of the world, but that thou shouldst keep them from evil' (John 17.15).[33] The presence of Christianity in the world gives rise to a twofold movement, each part of which divides into a prior dialectic of fact and a subsequent dialectic of thought. There is the movement of Christianity assimilating the world to itself, the work of the leaven that leaveneth the whole mass. There is movement of the world, convicted of sin yet refusing grace, in opposition to this intussusception of all things into the body of Christ. Further, the movement of Christianity may be a simple dialectic of fact, the spontaneous expansion through the zeal of apostles, the courage of martyrs (*sanguis martyrum, semen ecclesiae*), the moral beauty of Christian life. And similarly, the rejection on the part of the world may be a spontaneous movement of hatred: such as the fury of the Roman persecutions (Tacitus: *odio humani generis convicti sunt*;[34] Tertullian, Apol. 7: *coepit veritas, simul atque apparuit, inimica esse*);[35] and the liberal doubts about *odium fidei* as the basis of the persecutions not only have no foundation in historical science but argue a singular superficiality in human psychology. Again, there is the long interplay of static action and reaction, in which the church learns the value of philosophy from the definition of the *homoousios* through the Scholastic systematization of dogma to the modern elevation of St Thomas. On the other hand, during this same period the world builds up its dialectic of thought to arrive at Bolshevism as the one logical position for its resistance to Truth. Finally, there is the new apostolate and the new persecution. These proceed from the conclusions of the dialectic of thought. The church turns to scientific sociology and missiology. Sin turns to scientific propaganda, physical domination, moral perversion. Between these two contending forces, the *anēr pneumatikos* and the *anēr sarkikos*, lies the liberal idea of merely

33 NRSV: 'I am not asking you to take them out of the world, but I ask you to protect them from the evil one.'
34 *The Annals of Tacitus*, book 15; www. loebclassics.com/view/tacitus-annals/1931/pb_LCL322.285.xml; or: classics/mit.edu/Tacitus/annals.11. xv.html.
35 ML 1, 359.

natural man, the *anēr psychikos*, with no firmer foundation than actual fact and with no theory save a theory that ignores the two fundamental facts of original sin and the Incarnation.

[7 The meaning of history]³⁶

We now advance to our final conclusion, first examining the logic of our analysis of history, second asking, What is the meaning of history?

Our analysis is strictly philosophic. We lay down the theory of the intelligible unity and material difference of humanity; we divide the intelligible unity into a unity of nature and a unity of action; we demonstrate the unity of action from the principle of premotion; we explain the limitation of free will by noticing that the act of free will is either an acceptance of a rational dictate (and what reason dictates is predetermined) or the nonacceptance of the rational dictate (and what then happens is entirely predetermined). Perhaps it will be necessary for our outline of a *Summa Philosophica* to be read for the full appreciation of these philosophic points, particularly in what concerns freedom and the rationalization of sin. However, we legitimately assume here what we prove elsewhere.

Second, we study change in itself. We divide change into three kinds, according to its historic significance. First is the mere change of ordinary action: man lives as his ancestors. Second is the change that follows from the emergence of new ideas. Third is the change that follows from the emergence of systems of ideas, of philosophies. The first kind of change is of no interest. The second kind of change falls into three classes: ideas that understand the objective world; ideas that are vitiated by the existence of sin in the objective world; ideas that are elevated by the influence of divine revelation. In the third section we again have these same three divisions: but there is an essential difference. The ideas of the second kind of change are ideas in the concrete while those of the third kind are ideas in the abstract. The logic of ideas in the concrete is the logic of fact: it does not work out in pure thought but in the objective situation. Thus, the temple states of Mesopotamia and the city states of Greece had no unifying idea effective in the concrete: they were forced into an empire by the lack of such an idea, but this lack did not work out as a syllogism but by wars. Similarly, the empires were logically bound to fail for the lack

36 See Shute, *Options* 89–90.

of an idea that would integrate the differentials of change and progress in their far-flung territories: but Egypt, Babylon, and Rome passed away not by force of logic but by inner decay. On the other hand, the function of the applied dialectic of thought is to anticipate the need of the objective situation. Thus, the communist anticipates the breakdown of capitalism. The church executes a plan for the social order. The liberal was confident that *laissez faire* was an infallible recipe for the greatest happiness of the greatest number. The church, the liberal, and the communist bring about the objective social change not by ideas in the concrete but by ideas in the abstract.

It may be asked, especially of one who writes in English, 'What is the value of abstract ideas applied to the situation? Let us be practical.' The answer is that the abstract ideas have, indeed, a greater possibility of being wrong than the concrete ideas. Also, they work out for good or evil far more rapidly. But, whether we like it or not, the world has got beyond the stage where concrete problems can be solved merely in the concrete. Economics supplies us with the most palpable example: you have to have some economic theory in conducting the state, and changing from one to another with every change of government is neither intelligent, fair to the people, or fair to the wide world[,] which has to have a universal solution to the problem or go to pieces.[37] Politics supplies us with another example. The modern state does not think in terms of the past, of its merits or demerits in being what it is; it thinks in terms of the future, and if it foresees that it is being put out of the running by those with more economic power and more diplomatic skill, then it simply turns berserk in the name of Odin, Thor, or what you please. The sum and substance of the whole issue is that ideas in the concrete will build you a shanty but not a house and still less a skyscraper. The modern situation demands that questions be settled not in the concrete, not by the petty minds of politics who think of grabbing all they can because they can and make a virtue of not doing what they know either to be unprofitable or impossible, but in terms of pure reason. Physical reality functions perfectly in blind obedience to intelligible law. Humanity must first discover its law and then apply it: to discover the law is a long process, and to apply it a painful process, but it has to be done. The alternative is extinction. And practical minds are orientated towards extinction just as much whether they realize the point or not.

37 See above, p. 24, at note 19.

To return to history: From the point of view of the seven dialectics – the absolute *Geist* of revelation, which develops in its reaction to the world, the triple form of the dialectic of fact, and the triple form of the dialectic of thought – we do not pretend that these do not superpose and interact; on the contrary, that is their very nature. On the other hand, we may distinguish three distinct periods that view these dialectics from a different point of view. The first period was the development of mind by material need and social collaboration: it gave the world the idea of philosophy in Plato. The second period was the development of philosophy from Plato to the emergence of the idea of a social philosophy: this period continues till the need of philosophy as the prime mover in social life is recognized generally. The third period is the development of society under the control of a social philosophy: liberalism, the negation of any social philosophy, was the fact that makes a social philosophy a necessity of which men can be conscious; communism is [a] wild-eyed attempt to give the world such a philosophy; Catholic social theory has existed since the Middle Ages[,] but the degree to which Catholics were conscious of the importance of a social philosophy has been small almost up to the present time.

Again we digress to note the peculiarity of Catholic development. Catholic development is by reaction; but reaction may be mere opposition, or it may be higher synthesis. That much has been mere opposition was inevitable as long as Catholics did not grasp the significance of intellectual development and the necessary consequence of such intellectual development in social change: this failure of Catholics has always been a failure on the part of individuals. There were bishops who objected to the term *homoousios* because it was not in scripture; there were contemporaries to oppose St Thomas, who followed Aristotle and took the trouble to talk about the Arabs and refute them; there are Thomists whose last thought is to imitate St Thomas in this matter of thinking in pace with the times. Similarly, what is called anticlericalism is at root the antinomy between a merely traditional mentality and a mentality that is thinking in terms of the future and of problems of which the mere traditionalist has not the ghost of a notion, in fact, would flatly deny their existence, or, if they exist, that something should be done about it, or, if that is manifest, then that anything can be done about it. It is not indeed to be denied that the reactionary attitude has not a very firm foundation in fact, namely, in the very palpable fact that all the progressives are more or less in error, more or less perverse, more or less destructive. Nor is it to be denied that the reactionaries had any other course open to them in the past. You can protect the good either by simply sitting back or by advancing with the good; but to advance with the good you have to have a theory of progress and a will to progress; these were lacking.[38] Thus it is in the theory of social order, in the reestablishment of all things in Christ, in the leadership of Christ, King of the historical process, Prime Mover of the new order, that Pope Pius xi has laid the foundations for a triumph over an old, inevitable, and regrettable antinomy. For it is only in the philosophy of the church that can be attained the realization of that conception which Plato could not realize. It was true when Plato penned his *Republic*, but it is even more manifestly true today, that 'Men and cities cannot have happiness unless philosophers are kings.' To the world in its present plight of economic distress and political insecurity the church offers not philosophers but philosophy, nay, *hē hagia Sophia*, the Word made flesh, Truth consubstantial with the Father and the Spirit, as eternal King, as ruler of the historic process now that history has entered on its final stage of realizing abstract ideas.

We deduce the meaning of history from the intention of God's creating man as one, one in nature and one in action.

Creation aims at the manifestation of subsistential Wisdom, the Word. The angelic intellect is to the Word as the contingent to the Absolute; human intellect is to the angelic as potency to act. The contingent and the potential intellect are not merely mere participations of the absolute Wisdom but also are wisdoms in potency. To be wisdom in act they must meet with an act of love for the intelligible on the part of the will, *appetitus rationalis sequens formam intellectus*. But the will is free; you love because you love. To transcend freedom, creation divides into two parts. There is the angelic creation of pure individuals, specifically different from one another, and in this creation the good manifest Wisdom while the evil are the prime movers of sin in a world where there are not pure individuals but merely individuation by matter. In the material world, the manifestation of Wisdom lies in the triumph of good out of evil; because evil caused evil in the world, the world brings good out of this evil for a final vindication of good and a final triumph of the *Sapientia manifestanda*.

Because men are but one in nature and action, all the good in the world flows from the premotion of Wisdom and would not be were it not

38 See above, note 18.

for that premotion. On the other hand, all the evil in the world proceeds from its arbitrary basis of refusing the dictate of reason, [and] spreads by a dialectic of evil till evil is crushed by its own excess to give rise to a contrary and higher movement for still greater good. No flesh may glory in the sight of the Lord, for all good has its causation both physical and moral in the premotion of Christ. No evil can triumph, for every evil is permitted merely that good may more fully abound.

The role of the individual in the historic flux is twofold. Premotion offers him an intelligible dictate. He may accept, but his acceptance is not an act of his but simply an act that takes place in him: for the will naturally follows the dictate of reason; that is its *inclinatio naturalis*. He may not accept, but then he simply does nothing, for sin is *non-ens*, the failure of the will to act, something uncaused and inexplicable (because against reason), pure malice that is entirely his. This is regarding the individual from the viewpoint of the antecedents to his act or non-act. But the individual's act is not only a bracketed product of the past: it is a premotion for the future. The motion of the Prime Mover is passed from one individual to the next. Now, according as the individual acts according to reason or fails to do so, he decreases or increases the quantity of objective evil, of a disharmony between reason and objective fact in the world. Every individual is an instrument in the transmission of the premotion: but he may be an instrument for more sin or for less. He may be an instrument of sin or of Christ.

'Let not sin therefore reign in your mortal body, so as to obey the lusts thereof. Neither yield ye your members as instruments of iniquity unto sin: but present yourselves to God, as those that are alive from the dead; and your members as instruments of justice unto God' (Romans 6.12–13); cf. ibid. 6.19; 7.5–6.[39]

The meaning, then, of history is plain. It is the ever fuller manifestation of Eternal Wisdom first in a dialectic of fact and then through revelation

---

39 NRSV: 6.12–13: 'Therefore, do not let sin exercise dominion in your mortal bodies, to make you obey their passions. No longer present your members to sin as instruments of wickedness, but present yourselves to God as those who have been brought from death to life, and present your members to God as instruments of righteousness.' 6.19: 'For just as you once presented your members as slaves to impurity and to greater and greater iniquity, so now present your members as slaves to righteousness for sanctification.' 7.5–6: 'While we were living in the flesh, our sinful passions, aroused by the law, were at work in our members to bear fruit for death. But now we are discharged from the law, dead to that which held us captive, so that we are slaves not under the old written code but in the new life of the Spirit.'

in a dialectic of thought. The significance of the individual, 'endured with much patience as a vessel of wrath fitted for destruction ... or a vessel of mercy ... prepared unto glory' (Romans 9.22–23),[40] is to be a transmitting unit of the premotion of Wisdom or to fail in doing so, thus creating the growing evil of the world. The direction of the historic flow is an accelerating progress as man passes from the factual more and more into the reflective dialectic. The nature of progress is to reconquer through Christ the loss nature sustains through sin. For from original sin we derive a double evil: ignorance of the intelligible and difficulty in obeying the intelligible. The function of progress is to increase leisure that men may have more time to learn, to conquer material evil in privation and sickness that men [may] have less occasion to fear the merely factual and that they may have more confidence in the rule of intellect, to struggle against the inherited capital of injustice which creates such objective situations that men cannot be truly just unless first the objective situation is changed, and, finally – I am not certain I speak wildly – out of the very progress itself to produce a mildness of manners and temperament which will support and imitate and extend the mighty power of Christian charity. This, then, is the virtue of progress, the virtue of social justice, by which man directs his action so that it will be easier for his neighbors and his posterity to know and to do what is right and just. To this virtue are all men bound by the unity of human action, for the human act is twofold: an immanent rightness of will and an external transient rightness in the transmission of premotion. No man's achievement is his own: he is no more than a product of the past whether in the goods of the body or [in] the goods of the soul. No man's achievement is for himself: it is but a modification for good or evil of the premotion the world has from Adam and from the second Adam, Christ.

We sum up the significance of the external action of man in a citation: *divinorum operum omnium divinissimum Deo cooperari in salvatione animarum.* That is the significance of all our external acts. They are the activity of our members, and our members are either instruments of sin for greater sin or instruments of justice unto the justification of others. Man is one in nature and in action.

---

40 NRSV: 'What if God, desiring to show his wrath and to make known his power, has endured with much patience the objects of wrath that are made for destruction; and what if he has done so in order to make known the riches of his glory for the objects of mercy, which he has prepared beforehand for glory [...?]'

We have mentioned the fact that the greatest evil in the world is the evil that is concretized in the historic flow, the capital of injustice that hangs like a pall over every brilliant thing, that makes men and nations groan over others' glory, that provokes anger and suicide and dire wars, that culminates in the dull mind and sluggish body of the enslaved people or the decayed culture. The Christian counterpiece to this in the Christian's victory over sin is charity. For charity becomes not angry over wrongs, charity does not nourish hatred or threaten war, charity does not despair; charity is an eternal fire of optimism and of energy, dismayed at naught, rebuked by none, tireless, determined, deliberate; with deepest thought and unbounded spontaneity charity ever strives, struggles, labors, exhorts, implores, prays for the betterment of the unit action of man, for the effective rule of sweetness and light, for a fuller manifestation of what charity loves, Wisdom Divine, the Word made Flesh.

The Sovereign Pontiff has proclaimed the Kingship of Christ.[41] Do you know his kingdom?

'In the last days the mountain of the house of the Lord shall be prepared on the top of the mountains, and it shall be exalted above the hills: and all nations shall flow unto it. And many people shall go and say: Come, and let us go up to the mountain of the Lord and to the house of the God of Jacob: and he will teach us his ways and we will walk in his paths. For the law shall come forth from Sion: and the word of the Lord from Jerusalem. And he shall judge the Gentiles and rebuke many people: and they shall turn their swords into ploughshares and their spears into sickles. Nation shall not lift up sword against nation: neither shall they be exercised any more to war' (Isaias [sic] 2.2–4).[42]

Is this to be taken literally or is it figure? It would be fair and fine, indeed, to think it no figure.

41 On 11 December 1925, Pope Pius XI promulgated his encyclical letter *Quas primas*, on the Kingship of Christ. See below, p. 57, note 30.

42 NRSV: 'In days to come the mountain of the LORD's house shall be established as the highest of the mountains, and shall be raised above the hills; all the nations shall stream to it. Many peoples shall come and say, "Come, let us go up to the mountain of the LORD, to the house of the God of Jacob; that he may teach us his ways and that we may walk in his paths." For out of Zion shall go forth instruction, and the word of the LORD from Jerusalem. He shall judge between the nations, and shall arbitrate for many peoples; they shall beat their swords into plowshares, and their spears into pruning hooks; nation shall not lift up sword against nation, neither shall they learn war any more.'

2 *Pantōn Anakephalaiōsis*: A Theory of Human Solidarity[1]

'... oportet considerare quod intellectus noster de potentia in actum procedit. Omne autem quod procedit de potentia in actum prius pervenit ad actum incompletum, qui est medius inter potentiam et actum, quam ad

1 This selection is clearly dated at the end 'Dominica in Albis, 1935,' that is, 28 April 1935. The letter to Henry Keane mentioned in note 1 in the previous selection was written in January of 1935. In it Lonergan bemoaned the decadent state of Catholic thought at the time and expressed his hope of contributing to its renewal. The present paper shows even in its very title that it is intended to be a step toward the renewal that the letter asserts is so great a need.

The comments of Michael Shute on this selection may be found in *Origins* at 103–16. The work begins with a short preface or introduction, which is followed by the text proper. The typed pages of introduction were numbered at the top in the form, i), ii), iii), whereas the pages that follow are numbered in regular Arabic numerals, thus indicating that the preceding paragraphs were thought of as a sort of preface or introduction to the essay that follows. Lonergan's original manuscript is now available on www.bernardlonergan.com at 71306DTE030, together with our fourth selection, 'Sketch for a Metaphysic of Human Solidarity.' A version of this essay edited by Frederick E. Crowe and Robert M. Doran appeared in METHOD: *Journal of Lonergan Studies* 9:2 (October 1991) 134–72 and was relied on in editing the present contribution. Some of Crowe's editorial notes from that earlier version (170–72) were repeated here. References to those notes are specified simply by 'Crowe.'

actum perfectum ... Actus autem incompletus est scientia *imperfecta*, per quam sciuntur res *indistincte* sub quadam *confusione* ...'[2]

> *Pantōn Anakephalaiōsis*[3]
> A Theory of Human Solidarity
> A Metaphysic for the Interpretation of St Paul
> A Theology for the Social Order,
> Catholic Action,
> and the Kingship of Christ,
> *In Incipient Outline*

[Introduction][4]

Note: I trust the reader will be more inclined to be satisfied with suggestive ideas than to be exigent in the matter of logical development, exhaustive citation, careful exposition. The former is to some extent within the range of possibility for a student; the latter is not. Especially is this the case in the subject of this essay: for to write on the Pauline conception of our Blessed Lord as the *anakephalaiōsis* of all things presupposes very definite views on all things, theological, philosophic, historical, social, political, even economic. Now plainly it is one thing to justify one's

---

2 '... we have to consider that our intellect progresses from potency to act. But everything that progresses from potency to act arrives first at an incomplete act, one that is intermediate between potency and act, before arriving at perfect act ... Now [for intellect] an incomplete act is *imperfect* science, through which things are known *indistinctly* and with a certain *confusion* ...' Thomas Aquinas, *Summa Theologiae*, 1, q. 85, a. 3, c. The translation uses Lonergan's own terms, as they occur in the text; for example, 'progresses' for 'procedit.' The emphasis is Lonergan's.

3 The title is based on Ephesians 1.10, with a noun substituted for Paul's verb form: 'restoration' for 'restoring' (Lonergan's preferred translation) or 'unification' for 'to unite' [RSV] or 'gathering up' for 'to gather up' [NRSV]). 'Restoration' is not the perfect translation, but it is close to the Vulgate 'instaurare' and the Douay 'to re-establish,' both of which would be familiar to Lonergan, whose quotations are from the Douay. He himself used various terms: 'synthesis,' 'reunification,' 'integration,' and 'redintegration,' as well as 'restoration.'

   The column of Lonergan's titles is left as he typed it. His commas, introduced by hand, may show a hierarchy in the subtitles, which in fact are not all repeated in the heading Lonergan gave the body of the work: '*Pantōn Anakephalaiōsis*: A Theory of Human Solidarity.'

4 See Shute, *Origins* 92–93.

position in this multiple field of science and quite another to pluck as the fruit therefrom a synthetic view revealing the metaphysical convergence of all things on Christ Jesus, our Lord. On the other hand, the achievement of such synthesis constitutes of itself a manner of proof, proof that may be conceived in terms of Newman's integration of probabilities[5] or, more simply, in terms of the neat French phrase *la vérité s'impose*; on this ground, it will be seen, synthesis is to no slight extent independent of its presuppositions, and the procedure of this essay has an intrinsic justification as well as the extrinsic excuse of a student's manifold limitations.

The fundamental assumption of the essay is that a metaphysic is the necessary key to St Paul, as its fundamental contention is that the Thomist synthesis (pushed, indeed, to a few conclusions[6] which, if they seem new, may be regarded, I trust, as a legitimate development) provides such a key. The cardinal points of the conception we present are such as the theologian commonly fights shy of on the ground that they are too speculative to be of use to theology – a principle that would certainly have clipped the wings of St Thomas himself. Thus we make of capital importance the alternative of material and intelligible (by specific difference) individuation; we regard as a minor reality all potency, for potency is not an imitation of the divine essence but a condition for such imitation, which is to be found in essence and act alone; we argue that personality, as it is known to us, is the emergence of an intelligible individuation for which material individuation is a prerequisite (*materia propter formam*);[7] finally, we find this intelligible individuation in the actuation of intellect and will in human operation, and we synthesize[8] human operation in terms of the solidarity of human intellects and the statistical uniformity, as it were, of human wills. It is from the basis of a metaphysical conception

---

5 John Henry Newman, *An Essay in Aid of a Grammar of Assent* (London: Longmans, Green & Co., 1930) 288–92, 319–27, passim. Newman speaks regularly, not of 'integration' of probabilities but 'convergence,' 'cumulation,' 'summation,' 'combination,' or 'coalescence' of probabilities.
6 The rest of the bracketed phrase is a correction by hand of the previously typed 'that do not figure, at least prominently, in the current Thomist mentality.'
7 The notion of the intelligible individuation that Lonergan calls 'personality' is a major sub-theme in several of the documents in this section. See below, for example, in this essay pp. 52–54; in later essays, pp. 66, 70, 77, 79, 100, and 118 and see its anticipation in the first essay, above, pp. 6–7, 26, and 34.
8 Lonergan wrote 'synthetise.' The change is editorial.

of man, one in nature and operation, working through a material to an intelligible plurality in a transient dynamism in which no man is more than an instrumental cause and no causation fails to affect all men, that we attempt to interpret St Paul. This metaphysical conception we find to square accurately with the conception of humanity as an organism: the purely instrumental causality of man and the way in which this causality affects all men is exactly parallel to the purely instrumental causality of the members of a body and the way in which the operation of the members affects the whole body. This gives the *singuli autem alter alterius membra* of Romans 12.5.[9] But more; the principle of premotion makes these instrumental causes into a solidary chain of causation in which each instrument transfers the motion received from those before, transmitting it to those that follow; thus, a place of singular responsibility falls to the first mover among men, to the first and the second Adam. Adam corrupted the premotion and set up the reign of sin, a reign of disharmony and maladjustment in the corporate unity of man. Christ set up a new motion to harmonize, readjust, redintegrate a humanity that had reached the peak of disintegration and death described in the first chapter of Romans. This is the *anakephalaiōsis*. And it is in virtue of this new motion that men again live, live as though 'alive from the dead' [Romans 6.13], live 'yield[ing] their members as instruments of justice unto God' [Romans 6.13], live not indeed of themselves but only in virtue of the premotion according to the word: 'I live, not I, but Christ liveth in me' [Galatians 2.20]. 'Ita *multi unum* corpus sumus in Christo, singuli autem alter alterius membra.'[10] Thus, the material unity of man in Adam is replaced by the intelligible unity of man in Christ, the blind course of nature by the voluntary course of faith, the sinful course of the reign of a premotion from the serpent by the current of charity that has its formal cause in Christ as Wisdom and its efficient cause in the indwelling of the Holy Ghost as Love. Man is indeed made to the image and likeness of God when the actuation of his being is from the Father, the actuation of his adoptive sonship is from the Son, the Light of the world, and the actuation of his effective unity is from the Holy Ghost.

9 See the next note.
10 NRSV: '... so we, who are *many*, are *one* body in Christ, and individually we are members one of another' [Romans 12.5, emphasis added]; the English translations in the text are based on, but not entirely identical with, the Douay version.

In so vast a field of thought it is impossible to be complete; it may well be that I have defeated my purpose in attempting in so short a space so much; for the effort to include further aspects tends to give the impression more of audacious assertion than of sober speculation. However, let me do something to counteract this influence by expressing my willingness to go on any point to the *ultimum cur*. I append an outline of the argument.

1 Liberty as a disjunctive determination
2 The historical determination of intellect
3 The unity of human operation
4 The synthesis of human operation
5 The unity of man in the ontological ground of his being
6 *Pantōn Anakephalaiōsis*

Pantōn Anakephalaiōsis: A theory of human solidarity

1 [Liberty as a disjunctive determination][11]

The human will is an *appetitus naturalis sequens formam intellectus*.

(a) The form of intellect in question can be nothing but the dictate of reason, for the will is the faculty by which men not merely act but act reasonably; to follow the dictate of reason is to act well; not to follow it is to sin; the act of will is following this dictate; the non-act of will is the failure to follow this dictate; the non-act is sin.

(b) It is natural to man to follow the dictate of reason; when he does follow it, he is simply failing to do violence to his nature; hence, when we do all that is commanded of us, we remain unprofitable servants [Luke 17.10]. Plainly so, for to allow events to take their natural course, to permit one's faculties their natural operation and expansion, is not a title to merit but simply the absence of evil. Hence the Augustinian doctrine that sin is from man[12] and

---

11 See Shute, *Origins* 94.
12 'Nemo habet de suo nisi mendacium et peccatum' ['That which man has of his own is only falsehood and sin'] was an Augustinian doctrine given authority by the Council of Orange in 529 AD. See DS 392, with reference to Augustine's *In Evangelium Iohannis tract.* 5, 1. The same council repeatedly affirms the parallel Augustinian doctrine that everything else is from God.

everything else from God, who gives both the rational motives to our will and gives us wills naturally appetitive of rational motives: the naturalness of this appetite may be seen in the spiritual malady of remorse, which is the phenomenon of violence done the will.

(c) The non-act of will is the failure of the will to inhibit a motion that is contrary to reason: since only the will is free, it is clear that when the will does not act then the event is determinate, i.e., determined exactly as any other physical event.

(d) The act of will is the positive following of a dictate of reason: but what is reasonable under any given set of circumstances may be either objectively or subjectively reasonable. If objectively reasonable, then the human act of will is determinate in the order of pure reason. If only subjectively reasonable, then the human act is again determinate as a function of historical causation: for there will be a reason why this man does not know what is objectively right, and this reason why will lie in the field of history. This last point will become clearer later. As is plain, we may speak of objective reasonableness as equally due to historical causation.

(e) Hence human freedom is simply a choice between different determinate orders of events: if the will does not act, there is physical determination; if the will does act, then there is historical determination. Both are equally determined even though we cannot perform the psychological analysis necessary to prove the determination in that fashion, just as the distribution of the stars has some determining cause even though astronomy may be ignorant of it.

2 *[The historical determination of intellect]*[13]

We now proceed to investigate the historical determination of the form or dictate presented by intellect to the will.

(a) We first note that every act of intellect will be specified and so determined by a phantasm and that the phantasm has to be drawn from some historical situation. The historical situation gives the outer limits to what men can think about: what they actually will

13 See Shute, *Origins* 94–97.

think about will be discovered by proceeding to the limit, casting up the sum[14] of a man's momentum of interests, experience,
mental development, and actual position.

(b) Second, it is to be noted that every act of intellect is a universal.
The consequence is of importance in this inquiry, inasmuch as the
universal act of intellect will be a premise to an indefinite number
of acts of will. We are here at the root of the philosophy of history: the one act of intellect guides a man's many actions till it is
replaced by a contradictory idea; it guides not only the actions
of the originator but also all the actions of those to whom he has
communicated the idea either directly or by a secular tradition:
think of Buddha, Confucius. Further, the emergence of a contradictory idea is as much a determinate event as the emergence
of the first idea, for it has to be based upon phantasm and phantasms come from historical situations.

(c) Consequent to the relation between intellect and human act, one
act of intellect being capable of informing an indefinite number
of acts of will, is the following principle for the analysis of history:
the flow of human operations are [*sic*] determined by a single set
of ideas; a change in all the flow of operation follows from the
emergence of one new idea; the form of a flow of changes follows
from the form of the flow of new ideas, that is, from a purely logical dialectic. In mathematical terminology, abstract thought is the
second differential of human operation, while concrete thought is
the first differential.

(d) We arrive at the third differential by considering the form of human
thought as such. As St Thomas remarked, it is a progress from
potency to perfect act (perfect science from every viewpoint) through
a series of incomplete acts (*Summa Theologiae*, 1, q. 85, a. 3 c.).

---

14 Crowe, 170 note b, draws attention to Lonergan on summation many
years later: 'Intentional acts are summated into living: the accumulation
of experience, the acquisition of skills, of habits, of ways of doing things.
Objects are summated into situations, and the summation of situations is
the environment, the world, the horizon. Subjects are summated into the
intersubjectivity of community ...' Bernard Lonergan, 'The Mediation of
Christ in Prayer,' in *Philosophical and Theological Papers 1958–1964*, vol. 6 in
Collected Works of Bernard Lonergan, ed. Robert C. Croken, Frederick
E. Crowe, and Robert M. Doran (Toronto: University of Toronto Press,
1996) 170.

(e) It is to be noted that this progress from potency through incomplete act to perfect act is to be predicated not of the individual but of humanity. Perfect science does not exist yet; our science is an incomplete act of intellect. Further, it follows from the analogy of the angel, who in the instant (*aevum*) of his being solves all the problems relative to his specific nature, that man in the instant (*tempus*) of his being should solve the problems of his specific nature. Finally, the point is evident from the solidarity of human thought: the achievements and the errors of the past live on into the present and form the basis of the guidance intellect gives to will; with regard to this basis of traditional thought there is by the mass of men the application of the traditional principles to concrete situations and by the very few the addition of a new idea, a development or a higher synthesis of the old.

(f) Matter, the principle of individuation, isolates the individual from the unity of the species; but this isolation exists only for the sake of a higher unity, the unity of men by intellect. The exploitation of natural resources calls for a higher organization of men than the natural unit of the family or tribe; the organization gives rise to the need of political and juridical forms of society; the advance in the manner of satisfying physical needs at once exercises intellect, reveals its power, and gives the leisure necessary for the pursuit of culture, i.e., the development of the higher faculties of man.

(g) The unity of man achieved by intellect has to be a unity in truth, if it is to be stable. Peace fundamentally is this unity in truth, and only phenomenally is it *ordo cum tranquillitate*.[15] Opposed to peace is the atomization of humanity, the *Zersplitterung* that follows from error and sin, and the false substitutes of national self-idolatry or the deification of emperors to secure what reason is powerless to secure.

(h) There is in the natural order a threefold dialectic in the historic progress of intellect.

First, the dialectic of fact. The objective situation gives a phantasm which specifies an idea. The idea is an incomplete act of intellect, but it is

15 The reference may be to Augustine's 'tranquillitas ordinis,' *De civitate Dei* 19, 13.

put into execution as though it were complete: the result is a false historic situation which reveals the incompleteness of the old idea and leads to the emergence of a compensating idea.

Second, there is the dialectic of sin. False situations may be created not only by following incomplete acts of intellect as though they were complete but also by not following intellect at all. Thus, the depraved polytheism of the ancients arose from habit, which made sin seek an intellectual justification; similarly, the theory of liberalism is a consequent of the sixteenth-century heresy with the consequent religious wars, while the theory of communism is a consequent of the pharisaical religiosity of capitalist exploitation and oppression.

Third, there is the dialectic of thought. As a pure dialectic, it is the development of the *philosophia perennis* as new phantasms make a greater distinctness and precision possible. As contaminated with the dialectic of sin, the pure dialectic gives us the actual course of abstract thought since the emergence of philosophy as a human science with Socrates.

(i)   The potential character of intellect results through ignorance in an internal and external disharmony called concupiscence. The low *energeia*[16] of intellect leads men to believe that the sensible is the real, that is, the particular concrete object, which if accepted without qualification as the real leaves William of Ockham the *doctor invincibilis*. The fact that because of this potentiality men develop first as animals and very gradually come to the use of reason, when taken in conjunction with ignorance about reality, supplies the dynamic basis for concupiscence in the narrow sense; for it is under these circumstances that the subconscious development of nervous paths and patterns takes place in a way that later interferes with human autonomy over the flesh. Finally, the blunders and the sins of men create objective situations that should never exist and that easily become intolerable, whether we consider the microcosmic tragedies of passion and cruelty and suicide or the more terrible fruits of so-called economic and political forces.

16 Here, 'dynamism' would seem to be the preferred translation. See Crowe, p. 167, note 13.

3 [The unity of human operation][17]

What has been said of intellect reveals the unity of all human operation. The individual's intellectual pattern is determined by phantasms which come from objective situations containing both a tradition of past intellectual achievement and the data for future development. Any new idea is gestated by the situation of successive centuries, is brought to birth by some chance individual meeting the postulate of the situation, [and] immediately becomes the property of all affected by the situation as though the individual were but the instrument for general development. Thus it is that a first-year theologian today can solve the problem of baptism by heretics that left Cyprian and the early church utterly at a loss; and, on the other hand, it takes a Newman some fifteen years of very slow progress to arrive at the truth of Catholicism, so great is the all-pervasive power of traditional mentality. This point may be to some extent obscured to the reader if he thinks of the great variety of opinion at the present day: the fact is that at the present time we have not a burst of originality but the decay of intellect, the *Zersplitterung*, that results from men being out of touch with a tradition and fancying their primitively incomplete acts of intellect to be valid for the time; really, intellect has ceased to be a principle of unity among men; instead, we have the mass propaganda of national education, national newspapers, national morality, and the peace that comes of police, armaments, and forced military service. The nineteenth century's romantic liberalism in the cult of shoddy 'originality' might be tolerable if, as Bernard Shaw suggested, we went back to Methuselah[18] and men lived a millennium instead of dying off, as now, at the age of eighty when they are but beginning to have a few glimmerings of sense. But the providential dispensation that compensated for the patriarch's lack of tradition by longevity is merely fantastic as a solution to

---

17 See Shute, *Origins* 97–98.
18 George Bernard Shaw, *Back to Methuselah* (New York: Brentano's, 1921); from the preface: 'men do not live long enough; they are, for all the purposes of high civilization, mere children when they die ... If on opportunist grounds Man now fixes the term of his life at three score and ten years, he can equally fix it at three hundred, or three thousand, or even at the genuine Circumstantial Selection limit, which would be until a sooner-or-later-inevitable fatal accident makes an end of the individual' (pp. xviii–xix).

modern problems: modern men have to think in development of previous thought if they are to think at all.

The unity of intellect that follows from its potential character and the need of specification by phantasm results in an effective uniformity of will. Free will is but the choice between following the dictates of intellect and not attempting to control by reason the mere impulses of blind nature: it is a choice between two determinate orders. Moreover, there is a uniformity in this choosing. We speak of moral certitude with regard to the future free acts of men, and we recognize heroic virtue and inhuman vice as exceptions to a settled constancy. Thus, though the will is not determined, it remains that there is a statistical uniformity to the operations of will. In consequence, we may regard mankind as a machine of low efficiency that receives from the objective situation specifications of intellect and premotions but turns out operations that only in a certain percentage are according to intellect and the rest as if there was no intellectual control whatever.

We may conclude this section by putting the thought in the form of an argument. Men either think as they are taught or they think for themselves; in the latter case, they either bring forth ideas that are real advances in the field of intellect or they merely add to the atomization of humanity by proposing as true what is merely incomplete and false. In all three cases their thought is the thought of what may be called an objective *Geist*, the common mind of man: the traditionalist is merely another who thinks the same way, a numerical addition; the true originator is but the instrument for the advance of the objective *Geist*; the false originator is equally an instrument, not for advance but for destruction, the penalty of man's forgetting that he is but a member of a species and cannot do all the thinking of the species himself. Next, the good will that follows intellect does nothing but make the actions of man an instrument for fulfilling the practical aims of the objective *Geist*; on the other hand, the evil will makes human operation an instrument for the sub-intellectual determinate order. In either case, man is simply an instrument.

4 [The synthesis of human operation][19]

We may now attempt the synthesis of human operation. There is as the extrinsic basis of this operation the succession of nonhuman world events

19 See Shute, *Origins* 98–99.

in the physical and biological orders. As intrinsic basis there is the succession of individuals being born, begetting others, dying. In relation to both of these and to one another is the succession of human acts. Finally, arising from these three, controlling them, and being modified by them as a result of this control, is the succession of human thoughts, the development of the objective *Geist*.

Fr Portalié in his article on St Augustine in *Dictionnaire de théologie catholique*[20] considers the fundamental point in the Augustinian explanation of grace to be the psychological fact that man has not the initiation of his thoughts.

To a Thomist, this truth is self-evident. *Quidquid movetur ab alio movetur.* Will has to be premoved by intellect; intellect has to be premoved by phantasm; phantasm has to be premoved by an objective situation and environment; finally, the objective situation and environment is partly the determinate work of nature, partly the accumulated work of mankind acting now according to its limited knowledge and now against this knowledge.

Clearly, to a scientist with some highly refined mathematical calculus able to contemplate not only the multitudinous data of the problem but also the response of free wills to the precise intellectual forms that would arise from this complex scene, the whole course of history would be as simple and intelligible as is the course of the earth round the sun to a modern astronomer. It would be evident to this scientist that the principal cause of every event was the designer, creator, and first mover of the universe. He made the potencies what they are; set them in their intrinsic relations to one another; gave them their initial positions and their initial premotion; foresaw and intended the modification of position and of motion that would result as this premotion was transferred from one potency to another. What can operate only as the result of a premotion and only according to preestablished laws is simply an instrument, a machine; it does not cease to have a merely instrumental causality because of the freedom of selecting between the determinate order of an objective *Geist* and the determinate order of sub-intellectual operation. The omniscient sower who casts seed by the wayside, on stones, among thorns, is not surprised when he reaps no harvest there! A printer who hires men who use handpresses is as much the principal cause of what

20 Eugène Portalié, 'Augustin (Saint). Vie, oeuvres et doctrine,' in *Dictionnaire de théologie catholique* 1/2 (Paris: Letouzey, 1931), cols 2268–472.

is printed as the printer who buys more elaborate machinery and hires fewer men.

It is to be noted, however, that the *primum agens* uses human instruments to transfer his premotion and his predetermination. If you read a discerning autobiography you see a human life presented in terms of a number of influences from accidents of time and place and from other persons; now the lives of these influencing persons are similarly the product of previous influences; and so on till one gets back to the first man. Thus, while God is the principal cause of all operation insofar as he gave the initial premotion and predetermination and infallibly knew and deliberately intended all that would follow therefrom, the human instruments that transfer this premotion and predetermination differ from the physical or merely biological transference and instrumentality. For men by sin can make the motion to be transferred weaker; they can muddy the stream that descends to posterity. Man makes man. Man is his brother's keeper, for human operation is one operation, one successive transference of one premotion and one predetermination. Man is no more than an instrument, but he may be an instrument of righteousness or of sin; he may pass on to others what he has received, or he may pass on less; but he can do nothing else.

It is to be recalled that sin does not make man a principal cause of anything; sin is non-act, non-*ens*; it is not a motion or a causality but a failure to move and to cause; it is not a principal causality but an instrumental non-causality. On the other hand, when man does not sin, it is not because he is doing something of himself: the intellectual form was given him; the power of willing was given him; the premotion of will by intellect was given him; the act of will in response to the premotion of intellect is simply the spontaneous activity of the will in virtue of its *appetitus naturalis*; man does not add anything to the *appetitus naturalis* to make it go into act; he simply allows nature to take its course, does all that is required of him, and remains an unprofitable servant [Luke 17.10].

The reader may be unsatisfied with this; the reason will be that he considers there must be some act making the difference between the act of will and the non-act of will, some choice prior to both that is the true act of will.[21] This, I beg to suggest, is the fundamental blunder of the

---

21 Crowe, 171 note h: 'in his doctoral dissertation Lonergan will insist on the Thomist doctrine "that the objective difference between *posse agere* and *actu agere* is attained without any change emerging in the cause as such," and will comment: "To later scholastics this seemed impossible a priori: they

whole question. The non-act of will is *contra rationem*; when you try to *explain* what is *contra rationem* you try to make a contradiction intelligible; sin is the *unintelligible*, because it is *contra rationem*; and the explanation of the unintelligible is critical thought, the doubling back to the assertion that the explanation is the demonstration that explanation is intrinsically impossible. Do not confuse this with mystery: mystery is intelligible *quoad se* though not *quoad nos*; sin is intelligible neither *quoad se* nor *quoad nos*. Hence the good act is explained by the premotion from intellect and the *appetitus naturalis*; the evil act is unintelligible, intrinsically so, for it is the irrationality of a rational creature and a rational potency; to look for the reason of irrationality is absurd; did it have a reason, it would not be irrational; if sin had a reason or a cause, it would not be sin.

Finally, it is to be observed that I speak of the exclusively natural order. If man is merely an instrument in the natural order, a fortiori he is merely an instrument in the supernatural. But I am not speaking of the supernatural order; I am speaking as a psychologist of the school of St Augustine and St Thomas.

5 [The unity of man in the ontological ground of his being][22]

We now turn to consider the basis of the unity of human operation. Why are there economic forces making it impossible for industrialists to pay workmen a wage and for workmen to raise a family? Why are there political forces holding the world in the unstable equilibrium of a balance of power secured by *Realpolitik*?[23] Why are the sins of the monarchs and antipopes and reformers and enlighteners and Marxians visited upon the twentieth century in a measure so terrible that men refuse to face the plain

---

held that 'Peter not acting' must be really different from 'Peter acting.' They refused to believe that St Thomas could disagree with them on this; in fact, St Thomas disagreed." The present point is the obverse of that made in the dissertation: there the explanation of a cause acting, here the explanation of a cause not acting, in both the principle that causation does not involve any real change in the cause as cause.' See Bernard Lonergan, *Grace and Freedom: Operative Grace in the Thought of St Thomas Aquinas*, vol. 1 in Collected Works of Bernard Lonergan, ed. Frederick E. Crowe and Robert M. Doran (Toronto: University of Toronto Press, 2000) 72.

22 See Shute, *Origins* 99–101.

23 The word *Realpolitik* is inserted by hand, replacing the typed phrase 'unscrupulous diplomacy.'

facts of the situation? What is Adam to us that we should bear the penalty of original sin? What is the metaphysical principle of the Redemption? It is all one question, and it would seem to merit an answer.

The answer is that man is not simply an individual; angels are individuals; *man is never more than a member of a species*; he is not in his operation, as we have already demonstrated; he is not in the ontological ground of his being.

Philosophically, man is one universal nature *quoad id quod est*, and man is many merely in virtue of the modality of his being, *quoad modum quo est*. Man is one in virtue of his form, and he is many merely in virtue of matter, the principle of individuation of universal forms. The individual man really is an individual: *indivisum in se* and *divisum a quolibet alio*; but that reality is not pure reality but a compound of pure reality (what is participated of the divine essence) and a twofold potency, contingence and materiality, neither of which are in the divine essence, nor imitations of the divine essence, nor participations of the divine essence, but conditions of there being any imitation or participation of the divine essence besides the full possession enjoyed by the divine persons. Man as these many particulars is contingence and materiality; man as a universal nature is an intelligible essence and a limited aspect of the divine essence. Now as potency is because of act, it follows that the laws of mankind, that what is right and just for mankind, should proceed from the universal nature and be in terms of the universal nature and be irrespective of material difference.

Theologically, we may arrive at the same conclusion. Man is made in the image and likeness of God; the Father generates the Son in a generation, strictly so called; the Father and Son are consubstantial; therefore, men are consubstantial, not indeed in the same way as the Father and Son but in the image and likeness of that consubstantiality. Men are not strictly consubstantial but analogically so; they are different substances not *ratione essentiae* but *ratione materiae quantitate signatae*; but insofar as man fails to resemble the divinity, insofar he falls short of reality; and so the difference between men is less real than the unity of men.

This is a hard pill to swallow for those tending to be members of the '*invicta schola nominalium*'; but let us hear their arguments! Meanwhile, let us push further the analogy between the human and the divine.

First, we must distinguish between individuality and personality. I do not say between the individual and the person, since, *ratione suppositi*, these two are identical. I inquire into the difference between the *rationes formales*, individuality and personality.

Now a person is an individual with intellect and will. What is a personality? We argue as follows: the individuality results from matter, the principle of individuation; but matter is for the sake of some higher form; therefore, personality is the individuating form that can be brought forth in a material individuality by intellect and will. But what intellect and will bring forth in the way of an individuating form is a given – personal, as we say – orientation in life. Therefore, actual personality is the ultimate difference of intellectual pattern and habit of will called character that results from the operation of intellect and will in a material individual. On the other hand, potential personality is mere individuality with unactuated intellect and will. According to the measure of this actuation, we distinguish persons as majors and minors; on the analogy of an orientation of intellect and will in the individual, we speak of moral persons.

Second, we discover the reason for the continuous variety of the objective *Geist*, its differentiations in time as one idea is complemented by another, its differentiations in space as each individual arrives at a viewpoint that is the integral of the influences exerted upon him.

Third, we discover a moral personality emerging from the flux of birth and death and change, the moral personality of humanity, of the human race, the 'one and many.' For the personality arrived at by each individual is the product of previous personalities and the producer of future personalities: man makes man what he is, even though he does so as an instrumental cause that now acts and now fails to act. Thus there is in all men a responsibility and a debt to all men; no person is self-determined; no person fails to make things better or worse for the emergence of future personalities. This orientation of all men to all men is a moral personality.

Fourth, we complete our analogy to the Blessed Trinity. As the Trinity of Persons are subsistent relations in the eternal and equilibrated dynamism or *energeia* of unlimited intellect and will, so upon the transient dynamism of physical and biological nature emerge the physical personalities that should be the adoptive sons of God and the moral personality that should be the spirit of love for all men. In fact, human personalities are of three kinds: the *anthropos sarkikos*, who is orientated towards sensible satisfaction; the *anthropos psykhikos*, who is orientated towards the true, the good, and the beautiful; the *anthropos pneumatikos*, who is orientated towards God in his transcendence of the transcendentals and as he is known only by faith through revelation. Why are not all men in the last category? It is the fault of men. Why are graces sufficient but not efficacious? It is the fault of the human instruments whose duty it is to transfer to others the

motion they receive. Why does God draw some and not others? Because
he made man to his own image and likeness, one in nature and in operation, because he uses instruments to draw men according to the law
quidquid movetur ab alio movetur; because, finally, the instruments will not
be even unprofitable servants, will not live exclusively for his Truth, and
so cannot love as does his Love, will not love reason, the image of the
Word, and so cannot love man as did the Word. But the divine plan of
man in God's own image and likeness remains: persons that in an orientation of filial subordination to our Father in heaven constitute a moral personality of love for all men that all may be orientated to the Father of all.

6 [Pantōn Anakephalaiōsis][24]

We come to our final point, the *pantōn anakephalaiōsis*, the Pauline conception of the role of Christ in creation.

We have argued that, since man's operation is necessarily an instrumental operation, then there is a particular significance to leadership,
to being the first agent in human history. We set forth the fundamental
antitheses of the first and second Adam as follows.

(a) Adam, premoved by Eve, premoved by the serpent, set up the
reign of sin (Romans 5.12).

Christ, conceived by the Blessed Virgin Mary at the annuncia-
tion of the angel Gabriel, set up the kingdom of God.

N.B. The function of the angels is of importance for the cosmic
implications of the theory: we return to the point later.

(b) Adam communicates human nature to his progeny; parents are
quasi-instruments in the communication of Adam's sin, for they
communicate nature that no longer has something it would have
had if Adam had not sinned.

Christ communicates the divine adoption by regeneration of
water and the Holy Ghost; the church and parents are instrumental causes of this communication.

N.B. The difference between quasi-instrumentality of communicating sin and true instrumentality (however remote) in communicating grace lies in the difference between grace and sin: grace is
something, and sin is a privation of something; you do not commu-

24 See Shute, *Origins* 101–104.

nicate a privation of something, but communicate the something without communicating what is deprived.

(c) Adam and his progeny die the death that is the penalty for sin.

Christ transmutes death into the rite of sacrifice – greater love than this no man hath [John 15.13] – and makes of death the seed of resurrection, for he is *primogenitus ex mortuis* (Colossians 1.18).

(d) Adam by his forfeiture of the gift of infused knowledge reversed the course of history and set up the tradition of concupiscence. He reversed the course of history, for man had to develop from the mere potency of intellect, had to progress under the leadership of phantasms specifying intellect as chance offered them, became unable to plan progress but had to proceed in a series of more or less blind leaps of incomplete acts of intellect. This constitutes fundamentally, we have already argued, the ignorance and difficulty called concupiscence.

Christ restored the harmony of man by the grace of dogma, an absolute *Geist* above the wandering objective *Geist* of humanity. This point needs some expansion.

First, the coming of Christ coincides with the breakdown of philosophy and its recognized impotence to solve the problem of intellectual unity. Philosophy had to be discovered before Christ, else the Christian dogmas could not be expressed: prephilosophic symbolism led necessarily to idolatry; the Hebrews avoided it to some extent only by making the divinity inexpressible. Philosophy had to be bankrupt before Christ to make plain to man his impotence without Christ: even the philosopher emperors stooped to apotheosis.[25]

Second, the supernatural revelation to which Christ was a witness is not only a content but premoves a living and developing mind: the mind of the mystical body; 'we have the mind of Christ' (1 Corinthians 2.16). The patristic period only established the principle of despoiling the Egyptians: for instance, the bishops at Nicea who in the name of traditional mentality objected to defining the consubstantiality of the Son were overruled. This principle received its full application in Scholasticism, which did not fear to reason about anything and which so enriched ordinary

25 Handwritten alongside this entire paragraph are the words, 'cf Pauline "Impotence of the Law."'

Catholic thought that the early church with its misty conceptions on many points seems strange to us. The purely scientific character of the appeal to reason, as well as the definition of the limits of that appeal, was more than emphasized by the audacity of St Thomas of Aquin, who based his thought on Aristotle precisely because Aristotle's was the most scientific. Finally, the bull *Aeterni Patris*[26] was the official recognition of the social need of a philosophy, the necessity for human society that in some sense the philosopher be king, have a dictature over lesser minds and the *Zeitgeist*.

Third, the development of the absolute *Geist* through dogma[27] cannot be a development of the dogma, the revelation as such: that is a contradiction in terms, for the pure dogma is above reason. However, we may see in this development what the development of man's intellect would have been, had Adam not sinned. The development through dogma is not by the acceptance of incomplete acts of intellect and their factual refutation when put in practice (for example, economic science creating a world crisis); it is by the selection of what is true in the incomplete acts of intellect of the objective *Geist*; and this selection takes place in virtue of the light of the supernatural truth, in virtue of the illumination that proceeds from the Light of the world, the *Verbum Divinum*. What the progeny of Adam would have done through infused knowledge, we do through Christ our Lord.

Fourth, the intellectual benefit of the absolute *Geist* is something that man, fallen man with his fatal tendency to sensism and nominalism, easily overlooks. To those outside the church the endless intransigence of the church against heretics from the Gnostics to the modernists is incomprehensible; they prize moral goodness; they constantly forget that no man is better than he knows how; above all, they overlook the impotence of the traditional mentality (as opposed to the philosophic with its defined abstractions) to make issue with the expanding objective *Geist* of humanity; the breakup of Protestantism and the insolvency of the Orientals who call a dead tradition orthodoxy demonstrate which view is right. But there is more than this to the intellectualist position of the church: not

26 Encyclical of Pope Leo XIII, 1879, on Christian philosophy according to Thomas Aquinas.
27 A marginal note next to the paragraph probably belongs here: 'N.B. The development of dogma is the developed Absolute *Geist* turning back upon the content of revelation and seeing more there than was seen before.'

only is reason and the Thomistic canon *bonum hominis est secundum ratio-nem esse* the sole possibility of a catholicity that overrides the petty differences of nationality and other tribal instincts and therefore the sole possibility of a practical human unity; there are two further points. In the first place, any reflection on modern history and its consequent 'Crisis in the West'[28] reveals unmistakably the necessity of a *Summa Sociologica*. A metaphysic of history is not only imperative for the church to meet the attack of the Marxian materialist conception of history and its realization in apostolic Bolshevism:[29] it is imperative if man is to solve the modern politico-economic entanglement, if political and economic forces are to be subjected to the rule of reason, if cultural values and all the achievement of the past are to be saved both from the onslaughts of purblind statesmen and from the perfidious diplomacy of the merely destructive power of communism. But to establish the intellectual unity of men by appealing to reason is impossible; men refuse to be reasonable enough to take the League of Nations seriously, and that is too elementary a notion to be called a metaphysic. The only possible unity of men is dogma: the dogma of communism unites by terrorism to destroy; the dogma of race unites to protect, but it is meaningless as a principle of advance, and it is impotent as a principle of human unity; in plain language, it is not big enough an idea to meet the problem; it is a nostrum that increases the malady. There remains only the dogma of Christ. We have here the significance of Pope Pius xi's proclamation of Christ as King,[30] King as the rallying point for all men of good will, King of the historic process. We have here the significance of Pope Pius xi's proclamation of Catholic Action,[31] for Catholics are the leaven that leaveneth the whole mass. Finally, we have here the significance of Pope Pius xi's command that 'all candidates for the sacred priesthood must be adequately prepared ... by intense study of

---

28 See the explicit reference to Spengler below, p. 149.
29 An arrow is drawn from this clause to the margin, where there is written:
    'Had Hitler had something better than Gobineau and Chamberlain
    in the restoration of Germany, for instance!' Joseph Arthur Gobineau
    (1816–1882), French diplomat and man of letters, taught the inequality
    of humankind, only the white race being creative of culture; Houston
    Stewart Chamberlain (1855–1927), British-born political philosopher, who
    owed much to Gobineau, regarded 'Germanism' as the source of all that is
    best in European culture, and was an influence on Hitler. Recall the date
    of this writing: 1935.
30 Pius xi, 'Quas primas,' *Acta Apostolicae Sedis* 17 (1925) 593–610; DS 3675.
31 Pius xi, 'Ubi arcano Dei consilio,' *Acta Apostolicae Sedis* 14 (1922) 673–700.

social matters.'[32] This command has not yet been put into effect, nor can it be till there is a *Summa Sociologica*: without that we would only flounder in the blundering and false science that created the problem.

The second benefit of the absolute *Geist* as an intellectualism is that this is the natural means for man to overcome the evils consequent upon the low *energeia* of intellect, that is, the internal and external disharmony called concupiscence. For, first, it would seem that the sacraments are not intended to exorcise the evil; second, it would seem that concupiscence, being the extrinsic privation of an instrumental means to an end, can be overcome by Christ; third, it is evident that wise laws wisely administered and adapted do much to mitigate the external disharmony; fourth, it is evident that intellectual culture does much to blunt the crudity of passion; fifth, there is reason to believe that an intelligently ruled economic and the continued advance of science will give man much more leisure for the development of his higher faculties in the future than in the past; sixth, we are beginning to understand more of human physiology and of the subconscious activity of the soul on the organism so that a development of educational theory may enable man to solve problems he now views with all the scientific penetration of a Mongolian herdsman.

So much for the brief expansion we have permitted ourselves on the development of the mind of the mystical body and its expansion from the primitive tradition of dogma so as eventually to include a conscious body of social science illuminated by supernatural Light.

It is in this sphere of the role of the absolute *Geist* that Christ most luminously appears as *pantōn anakephalaiōsis*. By one man sin entered into the world, and in virtue of that one entry sin reigned. Now the reign of sin is a progressive atomization of humanity. Matter individuates man, and then man to overcome matter unites economically, politically, culturally, religiously; in every case, the basis of the union of men is an idea, an act of intellect; in every case, man is better off for having followed the idea; in every case, sin destroys the progress so that men are left with only the idea and without its fruit and come to look with suspicion on everything intellectual as a vain delusion. But it is not the idea that is to blame but the sin, the refusal to follow reason in all things. The idea is the principle of unity, but sin, acting contrary to reason, destroys the unity; the idea is a formal cause, but it must be joined with the effective causality of will to

---

32   Pius XI, 'Quadrigesimo anno,' *Acta Apostolicae Sedis* 23 (1931) at 226.

give effective unity, to give unity in truth whose phenomenon is the *ordo cum tranquillitate* called peace. Thus it is that the reign of sin culminates in that *Zersplitterung* of humanity described by St Paul: men 'foolish, dissolute, without affection, without fidelity, without mercy' (Romans 1.31). More could not be said.

Christ as the new head of humanity, as the reunification and redintegration of what is torn asunder by sin, is the originator of the absolute *Geist* of dogma, is the absolute of intellect in which participates the church, the *koinōnia*, the communion. For it is the absolute *Geist* of dogma that progresses without ever falling back; it is the Light of the world that selects the pure element of truth in the incomplete acts of the objective *Geist*. Next, intellect is the principle of human operation in unity; it is the principle of peace. But whether we read the Messianic prophecies, muse over the angels' hymn at Bethlehem, recall the discourse of the Last Supper, or turn to the texts in St Paul on the *anakephalaiōsis*, we always find the work of Christ described as the work of peace, the peace of a universal king, the peace that comes to men of good will, the peace that the world of sin with its balance of power and its economic imperialism cannot give. 'For in him all the fullness of God was pleased to dwell, and through him to reconcile to himself all things, whether on earth or in heaven, by *making peace* through the blood of his cross' (Colossians 1.19–20). 'With all wisdom and insight he has made known to us the mystery of his will, according to his good pleasure that he set forth in Christ, as a plan for the fullness of time, to gather up all things in him, things in heaven and things on earth' (Ephesians 1.8–10).[33] It is, then, the *mystērion* of the *anakephalaiōsis* that Christ is Plato's philosopher king. Plato saw the social necessity of philosophy, and before he died he renounced philosophy to play the ancient sage that gave men wise laws. But what Plato dreamt of, Christ would realize. The means are at his disposal. The church holds in check false speculation by anathemas; the church prevents the rationalization of making out that what is sin is no sin by imposing the obligation

---

33 Lonergan cited these passages in Latin. Colossians 1.19–20: 'Quia in ipso complacuit omnem plenitudinem inhabitare, et per eum reconciliare omnia in ipsum, *pacificans* per sanguinam crucis eius sive quae in terris sive quae in coelis sunt.' Ephesians 1.9–10: 'Ut notum faceret nobis sacramentum voluntatis suae secundum beneplacitum eius quod proposuit in eo, in dispensatione plenitudinis temporum, instaurare omnia in Christo quae in coelis et quae in terra sunt in ipso.'

of auricular confession; the church gives the human will the support of grace that flows through the sacraments; the church teaches the distinctive doctrine of Christ, which is charity, the only means of overcoming the evil of error and sin, the only alternative to the dialectic of sin, which takes objective evil as a premise and elaborates false principles as laws for the greater misery of mankind.

Christ is the *anakephalaiōsis* of humanity as the Light of the world, the principle of human unity, the prince of peace. But the *Verbum Divinum* is not only a source of intellectual light but also the object for the love of the will; for the will is *appetitus naturalis sequens formam intellectus*. From Christ by the sending of the Holy Ghost proceeds the active spiration in the human image of the Trinity; and in response to this active influence is the passive supernatural love of man, the theological virtue of charity.[34] 'Who then,' asks St Paul, 'shall separate us from the love of Christ? Shall tribulation? Or distress? Or famine? Or nakedness? Or danger? Or persecution? Or the sword? As it is written: For thy sake are we put to death all the day long. We are accounted as sheep for the slaughter. But in all these things we overcome, because of him that hath loved us. For I am sure that neither death, nor life, nor angels, nor principalities, nor powers, nor things present, nor things to come, nor might, nor depth, nor any other creature, shall be able to separate us from the love of God which is in Christ Jesus our Savior' (Romans 8.35–39). In this love, Christ is the center of the love which all men must have for all men in the unity of human nature and the solidarity of human operation. For to love one's neighbor and to love Christ is all one. 'Lord, when did we see thee hungry and fed thee: thirsty and gave thee to drink? And when did we see thee a stranger and took thee in? Or naked and covered thee? Or when did we see thee sick or in prison and came to thee?' (Matthew 25.37–39).

'Without me you can do nothing' [John 15.5]. This is true not only of the supernatural order of attaining the beatific vision. It is equally true of the social order; all things must be restored in Christ or there can be no restoration. For the twofold problem of intellectual unity and effective will is beyond the reach of man. Man is not willing to take himself

---

34 A very early expression of Lonergan's distinction of sanctifying grace and charity, with sanctifying grace associated with active spiration and charity with passive spiration. For the developed statement, see Bernard Lonergan, *The Triune God: Systematics*, vol. 12 in Collected Works of Bernard Lonergan, trans. Michael G. Shields, ed. Robert M. Doran and H. Daniel Monsour (Toronto: University of Toronto Press, 2007) 470–73.

as no more than an instrument. It is hard for him to see the truth of the alternative set him by St Paul: 'Let not sin therefore reign in your mortal body, so as to obey the lusts thereof. Neither yield ye your members as instruments of iniquity unto sin: but present yourselves to God, as those that are alive from the dead; and your members as instruments of justice unto God' (Romans 6.12–13). Man can choose only between the service of reason and of passion, only between the service of God or of sin, only between the Kingdom of Christ and the Kingdom of Satan. Man can be no more than an instrument. Man has to live as one alive from the dead, in a perpetual rite of sacrifice. Sacrifice, the shedding of blood, that is the whole meaning of life; and in this eternal oblation Christ is the *primum agens*. Let me close this aspect of our question with a citation from Donoso Cortés: 'Die Stadt Gottes und die Stadt der Welt ... stehen zueinander in schärfsten Gegensatz, nicht etwa weil man in der einen Blut vergiesst, in der andern nicht, sondern weil in der einen die Liebe das Blut vergiesst, in der andern der Hass.'[35]

(e) We now come to the final antithesis between the first and second Adam; this is at the same time the final synthesis of history, Christ as the formal cause and through the Holy Spirit the efficient cause of the end of all creation, the manifestation of divine wisdom in heaven as well as on earth.

First, we must ask why God did not create a universe in which there would be no sin, for obviously he could have created such a universe, and that irrespective of the liberty of creatures and the temptations they were subjected to. God has created those creatures that would sin. We ask why. The answer is well known: the divine wisdom in its transcendence of mystery and grace is better revealed when there are some creatures that

---

35 Cited by Erich Przywara in 'Dionysisches und christliches Opfer,' *Stimmen der Zeit* 129 (April 1935) 14. Lonergan gives part of the reference in his text, in parentheses. In translation: 'The city of God and the city of the world ... stand over against each other in the starkest contrast, not because blood is shed in one and not in the other, but because in one love sheds blood, while in the other it is hate that sheds blood.' See Lonergan's reference to and paraphrase of this statement in his review of Caryll Houselander, *This War Is the Passion*, in Bernard Lonergan, *Shorter Papers*, vol. 20 in Collected Works of Bernard Lonergan, ed. Robert D. Croken, Robert M. Doran, and H. Daniel Monsour (Toronto: University of Toronto Press, 2007) 150.

actually do sin; and it is not in the manifestation of divine justice by the punishment of sinners that this greater manifestation arises, for any penalty is a privation, and God does not reveal himself by negations, however terrible; the greater manifestation of divine wisdom lies in the need for grace that is created by sin. In the first place, there must be such a need: for God is intelligent and so cannot do things unnecessarily. In the second place, sin creates such a need. But this need is specifically different, as it were, in the sin of the angels and in the sin of man. The sin of the angels is in the case of each angel a purely individual sin, for each angel is strictly an individual with a specific difference from all the rest of creation: no one but himself is involved in the sin of each angel. The sin of man, on the other hand, is the sin of a potential individual that is not confined to the potential individual but, through the metaphysical unity that makes the many potential individuals one in nature and in operation, extends from the one potential individual to the nature and the operation of all the potential individuals. Thus the sin of Adam is, as it were, an anomaly: for in virtue of what man actually is (one nature potentially many individuals) reason requires that all sin in Adam; but in virtue of what man potentially is (many intelligibly distinct individuals proceeding from one nature) reason would require that not all sin in Adam. I say: 'Reason would require it.' The condition implied is that reason would require it, if the many potential individuals were not merely potential individuals; thus the condition is really an impossibility, a contradiction, for the many men can be intelligibly distinct only through their potentiality in the one human nature. It is on the basis of this quasi-anomaly that divine mercy finds an opportunity to intervene and bring forth the 'new creation' [2 Corinthians 5.17, Galatians 6.15] through Christ Jesus, a creation that in its transcendence of mystery and grace reveals the Word by the Word in a way that no single creation could achieve: to reveal the infinite there must be an infinite to be made issue with; infinite wisdom conquers the infinity of sin.

Hence as matter is for form so, in some analogous way, the sin of the first Adam is for the mystery of faith in Christ Jesus. But the Savior is not merely the supernatural pendent to Adam's infranatural sin: his significance is cosmic; he restores all things whether on earth or in heaven. Now this restoration of all things must be the final settling of accounts with sin. How is it such?

First, we note the peculiarity of a creature that is 'one and many.' The unity of human nature and operation – a unity that unfolds through a material to an intelligible plurality – is the connatural instrument for a victory over sin: for in this one nature and operation sin is not an isolated and instantaneous emergence of evil; it dilutes itself in time and spreads out into a reign of sin till sin culminates in monstrosity and topples over from its own enormity. Thus the antinomy of church and state, in modern times, through the dialectic of sin, became first the heresies, then the liberal states, and finally Bolshevik Russia, where sin in its pure form is organized by error, rules by terrorism, and attains security by the perversion of youth: the Bolshevik is ridiculous in his premise that man is merely an animal, but he is terrible in his power to make man merely an animal; and, if you blame the Bolshevik, you are blind: for Bolshevism is the social consequent of liberalism, and liberalism is the social consequent of heresy, and heresy is the social consequent of the opposition of church and state, and the opposition of church and state is inevitable as long as men are children of Adam – a predication that neither churchmen nor statesmen can avoid. (Is then the situation hopeless? Certainly, unless we settle down, face the facts, and think on the abstract level of modern history. But it is not in itself hopeless, for to God all things are possible even when he uses human instruments.)

Second, we note the solidarity between the sin of the angels and the sin of man. On the principle of *quidquid movetur ab alio movetur* it would have been impossible for Adam to think of sinning unless the serpent had intervened to tempt him through Eve. Adam was not as we are; he was not ignorant; he was not weak; he suffered no premotion contrary to his nature; the premotion to sin had to have an extrinsic origin. Thus the reign of sin on earth takes its origin in the father of lies; Adam by sin made himself the instrument of Satan's premotion; the reign of sin is the reign of Satan and a terrestrial repercussion of the sin of the angels; therefore, the kingdom of God, Christ, the Messsianic King, the Prince of Peace, the Eternal High Priest and Victim, the Light of the world and the *Primum Agens* of the reillumination of man, through the *plerōma* of the achievement in his first advent,[36] shall in his second advent finally settle all accounts with sin whether on heaven or on earth.

'He is the head of the body, the church; he is the beginning, the first-born from the dead, so that he might come to *have first place* in everything. For in him all the fullness of God was pleased to dwell, and through

---

36 See Ephesians 1.23, 3.19, 4.13; Colossians 1.19, 2.9.

him God was pleased to reconcile to himself all things, whether on earth or in heaven, by *making peace* through the *blood* of his cross' (Colossians 1.18–20).[37]

Palazzo Borromeo, Dominica in Albis, 1935
Bernard J.F. Lonergan, S.J.[38]

37 Lonergan cited this passage in Latin. Most of it can be found above in note 17.
38 The signature and indication of place are handwritten. Palazzo Borromeo was the Jesuit seminary in Rome, Via del Seminario, 120, for students in basic philosophy and theology; after the war, when it was called Collegio Bellarmino, it became the international house for Jesuit graduate students. In the year of this essay it was a community of 103, with about ten countries represented. Dominica in Albis: the first Sunday after Easter, and therefore 28 April in 1935.

3 *Pantōn Anakephalaiōsis* (2)[1]

1 Our aim is to outline the metaphysic of human solidarity that is more or less implicit in the epistles of St Paul.[2]

2 We distinguish two kinds of consubstantiality: real and imitative. Real consubstantiality is the consubstantiality of the Divine Persons. Imitative consubstantiality is the consubstantiality of beings with the same nature communicated from one to the other but resulting in a real and substantial difference from individuation by matter.

The *ratio theologica* is in Genesis 1.26: 'Let us make man to our image and likeness'; and in the theological thesis that the generation of the Word is *generatio proprie dicta*.

The *ratio philosophica* lies in the doctrine of universals. Man is one *quoad id quod est*, for he is a universal nature and only one universal; man is

---

1 To the right of this title, Lonergan wrote by hand: 'in terms of about 20 ideas, not proved!!' The paper is a summary statement of the major proposals presented in the previous entry in this volume. The comments of Michael Shute on this selection may be found in *Origins* at 105–107. Shute grants that there is not a lot of evidence to determine which was written first, but he concedes (106) that the present essay may have been composed somewhat later. Lonergan's original manuscript is available on www.bernardlonergan.com at 71303DTE030.
2 Lonergan added by hand: 'More outline than metaphysic, but as St Thomas would say, we progress from the general and the vague to the precise and clear.'

many only by a mere modality of his being, *quoad modum quo est*; further, the difference in man is lower than the unity, for the unity proceeds from the form while the difference proceeds from matter.[3]

3   We distinguish individuality and personality. Individuality is the being *unum in se et diversum a quolibet alio*. Personality is the individuality that belongs to intelligent beings.

We distinguish potential and actual personality. Potential personality is the mere possession of individuality, intellect, and will. Actual personality is the actuation of intellect and will sufficient to give a final and quasi-autonomous orientation in action to the individual.[4]

4   We distinguish three forms of personality, orientation in life.

The *anthropos sarkikos* is orientated to the external world of sense; he is in a relation of effective subordination to it, though in his own mind he may think he is subordinating the external world to himself. But he errs in this, for his thought is entirely conditioned by the external, and over that he ultimately has no control; he may exploit for a while – but read Wolsey to Cromwell in Henry VIII.[5]

The *anthropos psychikos* is orientated in a relation of subordination to the transcendentals of the True, the Good, and the Beautiful. He represents human nature at its best.

The *anthropos pneumatikos* is orientated in a relation of subordination to God as he is in himself, i.e., as transcending the transcendentals, as known only through revelation and by faith.

5   Man is *in genere intelligibilium ut potentia*, i.e., his intellect passes through a series of incomplete acts on its way to the perfect act of .

3   Lonergan added by hand: 'If you ask what man is this "one" and "many," I answer that either you are a nominalist or you cannot answer William of Ockham and so should be a nominalist. This is only a *boutade*, but I cannot argue the point here.'
4   Lonergan added by hand: 'Personality : individuality :: form : matter. *Materia propter formam*.'
5   A reference to Shakespeare's *Henry* VIII, and probably to Cardinal Wolsey's attempts at the end of Act 3, Scene 2, to give his protégé Thomas Cromwell some good advice so that he doesn't make the same mistakes that Wolsey made.

the human intellect, which is perfect science (*Summa theologiae*, 1, q. 85, a. 3 c.).[6] Further, as the angel, *in genere intelligibilium ut actus*, solves all the problems of his specific world in the instant (*aevum*) of his being, so man, the one human nature, solves all the problems of his specific nature in the instant of his being: only that instant is all time.

We note that had Adam not sinned then man would not have had to progress in the blind fashion in which he does as a result of the fall. Intellectual advance is now conditioned by chance discovery; the progress of man is not a planned and orderly whole but a series of more or less blind leaps. In other words, were it not for the fall, man would not have begun his progress from the 'scratch' of mere potency.

6   The human will is *appetitus naturalis sequens formam intellectus*. The human will is both premoved and prelimited. It cannot act without a previous dictate from intellect. It can act only in response to a previous dictate of intellect. But it need not act: this is its freedom, the freedom of the non-act, not following reason, not inhibiting the tendency that is contrary to reason.[7]

I cannot here give my demonstration that this is the precise nature of the human will.[8] Suffice to recall Aristotle's contention that the world would be better were it not for human liberty: that is, it would be more orderly, for reason would always be followed as in inanimate or brute nature; but it would be lower in kind.

7   With one exception, the human intellect is predetermined in the form that it presents to the will; this exception arises from the undue influence of the will. For man's intellect acts only with reference to a phantasm, and phantasms are all predetermined, with the restriction due to the influence of the will.

6   See also Thomas Aquinas, *Summa theologiae*, 1, q. 87, a. 1.
7   In the margin next to this paragraph, Lonergan wrote: 'Principles: (1) Quidquid movetur ab alio movetur. (2) Voluntas non movetur nisi a dictamine rationis.'
8   This paragraph starts a new page. Above it is written: 'N.B. No actus humanus indifferens [no human act is indifferent]. No free act that is not an actus humanus.' On 'actus humanus' see below, p. 98, note 5.

The influence of the will is to cause error. (We prescind from 'faith.')
There is the error of undue haste and ignorance of logic: this we may
reduce to the category of determinate events, for man has to learn not to
be hasty and not to be ignorant of logic. There is the error of rationalization. This error in its ultimate form is that referred to by St Paul when he
remarks: 'they would not have God in their knowledge' [Romans 1.28].
In itself, this error consists in making out that sin is not sin: everyone is
guilty of this to some extent, and so the best example is the religious who
makes futile excuses to himself for not observing his rule rigorously.⁹

8 We now advance to the pure theory of the unity of human operation. Man is one in nature. He is also one in action. We establish
   this by establishing the unity of human intellect and the statistical
   uniformity of the human will.

The basic principle is *quidquid movetur ab alio movetur*.
The general thesis is that human action is never more than the action
of a *causa secunda et instrumentalis*, the action of transferring a given premotion from a *primum agens* on to other individuals who transfer it still
further on till the ultimate fullness of time (*Summa theologiae*, 1, q. 105,
a. 5 c.).

9 We note that the man with the original idea is the exception and
   not the rule. Men think exactly as they are taught to think, or they
   rebel to fall in line with the doctrine of some other teacher. Now
   where do the ideas come from? What is the law of their emergence?¹⁰

In the first instance, man's ideas are discoveries for the better satisfaction of his material needs. The possibility of invention is restricted by its
practicability. Any such invention is readily communicated.¹¹
In the second instance, man's ideas arising from the exploitation of
natural resources lead to the organization of man in social forms higher
than that of the family or tribe.

9 In the left margin, Lonergan wrote: 'The Platonic "lie in the soul."'
10 Compare the seven 'instances' that follow with the phases of history above,
   pp. 11–24.
11 This sentence was added by hand.

In the third instance, we have the birth of the mechanical arts and of the sciences supported by the division of labor.

In the fourth instance, we have the development of culture about the symbolic expressions of the divinity – which are the only possible expressions before philosophy. N.B. Idolatry among Hebrews and Gentiles.

In the fifth instance, we have philosophy and the failure of philosophy to set up an ideal Republic, i.e., the rule of reason – long since corrupt.

In the sixth instance, we have the disintegration of philosophy in a set of equally insignificant schools as far as society is concerned. All are not equally bad, but all are equally ineffective.

In the seventh instance, we have each man thinking as he pleases and society in a dry rot ready to be torn to pieces by mere passion: for peace is unity in truth, and without truth there is no unity; men disintegrated by matter can be united only by truth.

10   We note a triple dialectic in the development of the human intellect.

There is the dialectic of fact. An incomplete act of intellect is made a guiding norm of human action. A false situation is set up which reveals the incompleteness of the act of intellect and emphasizes its shortcoming. A new idea is brought to birth and readily accepted to solve the problem.

There is the dialectic of sin. This is the process of rationalization, whether carried out in the minds of a number of individuals – e.g., the depravation of ancient polytheism, the *odium fidei* that gave rise to the early persecutions – or carried out by abstract thought upon a situation which should never have arisen but actually did arise by sin. Since the situation is false, the facts arising from the error and material sin will be evidence for what is false: thus, the religious wars gave birth to liberalism, the pharisaical religiosity of the capitalists to communism, the extravagance of the autonomy of states to the mad nationalism of our time, the Caesaropapism of Protestantism to a divorce between intellect and religion as the normal course of human life.

There is the dialectic of the absolute *Geist* (cf. 1 Corinthians 2.16).[12] This is the development of dogma, selecting what is true in the development of the objective *Geist* of humanity and rejecting what is false in the

12 '"For who has known the mind of the Lord so as to instruct him?" But we have the mind of Christ.'

incompleteness of the acts of progressing intellect. It represents the complete antithesis to the dialectic of sin: it prevents rationalization of sin by confession; it preserves truth by anathemas; it meets objective evil not by theories with sin for a premise but by charity, the only solution.

One may distinguish a prephilosophic and a philosophic period in the progress of the human intellect. In the former, the logic of fact is allowed to work itself out: false economic theory to a world crisis, etc.; in the latter, philosophy is accepted as a social norm, and the philosopher becomes king, in some sense.[13]

11   We recall what we laid down about the premotion and prelimitation of the human will (§ 6). The following aspects call for attention.

The act of will as an immanent act is the actuation of a personality, i.e., of an individuation that is independent of matter.

The act of will as a transient act is the control of the transient operations of man: if the act is reasonable, it leaves the objective situation orderly; if it is unreasonable, it is a contribution to objective disorder: hence, oppression, cruelty, suicide, wars, misery of all kinds, ignorance, error set up as truth.

Thirdly, since no man is better than he knows how and no man can be worse than his opportunities, we arrive in the limiting case of the concrete situation at all but a predetermination.

Fourthly, although we do not arrive at a predetermination, for man need never be reasonable,[14] it remains that there is a statistical uniformity of human wills. Men turn out in much the same proportion of good or bad. What makes one epoch worse than another is the quantity of error that is imposed by a tradition.[15]

12   Human liberty amounts to no more than not sinning. If man does not sin, then all is orderly and works out according to an orderly plan of development.

---

13 Added by hand: 'e.g. St Thomas in Catholic thought – yet *vetera novis augere et perficere* Leo XIII.'
14 The words from 'for' are added by hand.
15 Added by hand: 'cf. Moral certitude, heroic virtue, inhuman vice.'

Since *quidquid movetur ab alio movetur*, it is impossible for any good act not to be the product of the objective situation illuminated by reason. The evil act is simply the failure of the will to inhibit the lower determined order of sense.[16]

Since the objective situation is nothing but the accumulated action of man in the past, and man's action in the past was similarly determined, we arrive at the conception of human action being the transmission of a premotion from a *primum agens*.

The freedom of man with regard to this premotion means that man gives his members as *instruments* to the transmission of truth and goodness or as *instruments* to swelling the flow of sin. No more. Romans 6.13, 6.19, 7.5–6.[17]

Finally, when man does what is right, he is simply not destroying the objective order, he is an unprofitable servant, receiving a premotion to good and not opposing and nullifying it.[18]

13   Since the whole of human operation is reducible to the trans-
     mission of the premotion of a *primum agens* through a statisti-
     cally determinate development of intellect, we recapitulate or
     synthesize[19] or know in its intelligibility the whole operation of
     the one human nature by considering the primal agency. It is
     twofold. We set it forth in the antitheses of the first and second
     Adam, the natural head of humanity and the head of the mysti-
     cal body.

16 This sentence was added by hand.
17 The scripture references are added by hand in the margin. Romans 6.13:
    'No longer present your members to sin as instruments of wickedness, but
    present yourselves to God as those who have been brought from death to
    life, and present your members to God as instruments of righteousness.'
    Romans 6.19: 'For just as you once presented your members as slaves
    to impurity and to greater and greater iniquity, so now present your
    members as slaves to righteousness for sanctification.' Romans 7.5–6:
    'While we were living in the flesh, our sinful passions, aroused by the law,
    were at work in our members to bear fruit for death. But now we are
    discharged from the law, dead to that which held us captive, so that we are
    slaves not under the old written code but in the new life of the Spirit.'
18 The last part of this sentence, from 'receiving,' was added by hand. Lonergan
    continues by hand: 'Cf. Augustine *passim*: Good act exclusively from Christ
    (the necessary premover); evil act as evil exclusively from bad will of sinner (at
    least as presented by Portalié in DTC).' On Portalié, see above, p. 49, note 20.
19 Again, Lonergan wrote 'synthetise.' See above, p. 40, note 8. The change
    is editorial.

(a) Adam premoved by Eve premoved by the serpent set up the reign
     of sin. Romans 5.12.

     Christ conceived by the Blessed Virgin Mary at the annunciation of
     the angel set up the kingdom of God.

(b) Adam communicates fallen human nature by generation; parents
     are instrumental causes in his communication of nature as fallen;
     Adam is the principal cause in the communication of nature as
     fallen; God is the principal cause in the communication of nature
     simpliciter.

     Christ communicates the divine adoption by regeneration of water
     and the Holy Ghost: the church and Catholic parents are the instru-
     mental causes of this communication.

(c) Adam and his progeny die the death that is the penalty for sin.

     Christ and his progeny die the death of sacrifice, the greatest act
     of love; this death is the seed of the resurrection, and Christ is *primo-
     genitus ex mortuis* (Colossians 1.18).

(d) Adam by sin deprives man of the gift of integrity: i.e., an inter-
     nal disharmony from the low *energeia* of intellect and an external
     disharmony arising from the false and evil situations produced by
     actual sin and ignorance and stupidity.

     Christ restores the internal harmony by actual and infused graces
     and virtues; he also restores the external harmony, for the church is
     the leaven that leaveneth the whole mass, and Christ is King of the
     social order, the Messias and Prince of Peace.

(e) The reign of sin is a progressive disunity: man individuated by
     matter is united by intellect (economics, politics, culture, reli-
     gion); sin, acting against reason, destroys the unifying principle
     of human operation; you can do nothing with people who will
     not listen to reason, and you can do nothing at all after they
     have had the running of things and landed them in an inextri-
     cable mess.

The kingdom of God is the reunion, the redintegration of humanity, the restoration of 'unity in truth'; peace as *ordo cum tranquillitate* is the phenomenon of this 'unity in truth.' Hence Christ is spoken of as *pacificans omnia* in Colossians 1.20; he speaks of his peace which the world cannot give; he leaves and gives this peace, promised by the choirs over Bethlehem to men of good will; he teaches the one way in which the problems produced by sin can be solved, i.e., not by theorizing with sin for a premise but by charity.

(f) The premotion of Adam is to the premotion of Christ as matter to form.

Adam is the natural head of man, first in the order of time, of involuntary generation, of mere individuality, of sin.

Christ is the supernatural head of man, first in the order of nature, of voluntary membership of an intelligible unity in a society, of the personality of the *anthropos pneumatikos*, of grace.

All of these are related more or less as matter or empirical precondition to form or intelligible fulfilment.

But more. Adam's sin was part of the divine plan, for God could have created a world in which there was no sin. Why then did he so create? Because the end of creation is the manifestation of the divine wisdom, the Word, in its transcendental incomprehensibility of mystery and grace. The actual course of this manifestation has been: the angels sinned (for refusing to adore the Babe of Bethlehem [?]);[20] their sin was individual. Adam sinned, though he could not have thought of doing so without the premotion from the serpent. But the sin of man was different from the purely individual sin of the angels; man is one in nature and in operation; the sin of man endures and expands in the objective situation till in its enormity it topples over to bring forth by reaction a greater and intenser good of wisdom and charity. Since, then, humanity is one in nature and operation, sin in humanity is not a pure loss, an absolute deficit; rather it is a contribution to the production of one, essentially one, greater glory of God. In then this final balancing of accounts, Christ is in all things holding the first place.

Quidquid movetur ab alio movetur. What would human history have been without Christ? Europe without the faith? Like Asia only worse! When St

---

20 The question mark in brackets is in Lonergan's text.

Paul says, 'I live, not I, but Christ liveth in me,' he does not speak of extraordinary sanctity, necessarily. Every man, insofar as he lives at all, lives in virtue of Christ's premotion, does not prevent and nullify the intellectual forms that come to him from Christ from being of effect. At the coming of Christ men were 'foolish, dissolute, without affection, without fidelity, without mercy.' It is a historical fact even without the testimony of St Paul. Where does the difference come from? From Christ alone. Read Plato, and you know the impotence of humanity to solve the problem created by the dialectic of sin. Plato saw the better and approved but could do nothing; Aristotle wrote a practical ethic, something that like Stoicism helped men to endure life, but did not teach mankind to live it.

14 We return to the fundamental thesis: 'Let us make man to our own image and likeness.' We saw in the fact of generation the primary likeness to the Trinity. We have been paving the way for the second.

The three divine persons are the relations subsisting in the immanent dynamism of unlimited intellect and will.

Man is a transient dynamism of intellect and will based upon a material flux. The production of every personality is the corporate work of the individual and his predecessors. Read Newman's *Apologia* or any discerning autobiography: you see the individual to be what he is because he was the subject of a number of influences from others; and this is true of every individual. Man makes man what he is in a continuous succession of emerging individuals.

Hence besides the physical personalities of humanity, there is also the moral person of solidary humanity; this moral person is the person responsible for all the physical personalities; responsible, for man makes man, for there is such a thing as social justice, the justice that is justice to humanity, the justice that is opposed to the exploitation and oppression which sets up situations in which the right is impossible (e.g., impossibility of paying a just wage, of having a family, of avoiding a cataclysmic war).

Man, the many, is the generation of the adoptive sons of God.

Man, the one, is the emergence of universal charity: the love of Christ and the love of all men in Christ. Romans 8.35; Matthew 25.34–36.[21] The

21 Romans 8.35: 'Who will separate us from the love of Christ? Will hardship, or distress, or persecution, or famine, or nakedness, or peril, or sword?' Matthew 25.34–36 presents the words of the king to those at his right hand.

spiratio between the principal and the instrumental causes in the generation of the adoptive sons of God is from the part of the principal cause the sending of the Holy Ghost, and from the part of the instrumental cause the exclamation of St Paul: Who then shall separate us from the love of Christ? And this love of Christ is the love of the least of these, his little ones. It is the love of social order, the condition that the least may live and learn to know and to love him. 'He is the head of the body, the church; he is the beginning, the firstborn from the dead, that in everything he might have first place. For in him all the fullness of God was pleased to dwell, and through him to reconcile to himself all things, whether on earth or in heaven' (Colossians 1.18–20). '... he has made known to us the mystery of his will, according to his good pleasure that he set forth in Christ, as a plan to gather up all things in him, things in heaven and things on earth' (Ephesians 1.9–10). 'We know that the whole creation has been groaning in labor pains until now; and not only the creation, but we ourselves, who have the first fruits of the Spirit ...' (Romans 8.22–23).[22]

22 Lonergan cited these passages in Latin, and entirely in upper-case letters. Colossians 1.18–20: 'Et ipse est caput corporis ecclesiae qui est principium primogenitus ex mortuis ut sit ipse in omnibus primatum tenens. Quia in ipso complacuit omnem plenitudinem inhabitare et per eum reconciliare omnia in ipsum pacificans per sanguinem crucis eius sive quae in terris sive quae in coelis sunt.' Ephesians 1.9–10: '... ut notum faceret nobis sacramentum voluntatis suae secundum beneplacitum eius quod proposuit in eo (in dispensatione plenitudinis temporum) instaurare omnia in Christo quae in coelis et quae in terra sunt in ipso.' Romans 8.22–23: 'Scimus enim quod omnis creatura ingemiscit et parturit usque adhuc. Non solum autem illa sed et nos ipsi primitias Spiritus habentes.'

4 Sketch for a Metaphysic of Human Solidarity[1]

1 The real is exhausted by the terms 'existence,' 'individuation,' 'essence'; i.e., everything that is *exists* as a *particular* of a certain *kind*.
2 Existence is either intelligible or empirical.

Intelligible existence is the existence *per se nota quoad se*. Empirical existence is the existence that is not *per se nota quoad se*. Empirical existence does not exclude all intelligibility: it is not intelligible in itself; to be known it has to be known as a matter of fact, empirically; once it is so known, it may be understood, but not in terms of itself but only in terms of a purely intelligible existence.

Empirical existence is also called contingent.

Empirical existence is what is called the *suppositum*, i.e., what is presupposed to exist by intellect in its pure discourse; pure discourse *quoad se* could treat of God, it could treat of human nature, it could treat of an *n*-dimensional space; the existence of the last two, however, has either to be presupposed or to be prescinded from by pure discourse; on the other hand, pure discourse *quoad se* includes the existence of God.

---

1 The comments of Michael Shute on this selection may be found in *Origins* at 108–109. A summary statement regarding the first four selections may be found at 109–10. Shute tentatively suggests 1935 as the year of composition for this selection. Lonergan's original manuscript is available in digital form at 71306DTE030 on www.bernardlonergan.com.

It is in the order of empirical existence that the axiom holds: *quae sunt eadem uni tertio sunt eadem inter se*. Thus, this intellectual and this sensible are really one thing; they are really one thing empirically, as a matter of fact, because they are both found in the one contingent being though either may be found separately in contingent beings (angels and animals). On the other hand, this principle has a strictly limited application in the order of purely intelligible existence, i.e., the Blessed Trinity.

3 Individuation is either intelligible or empirical.

Intelligible differentiation is in virtue of an intelligible difference: thus, the Father differs intelligibly from the Son according to the opposition of the relations; similarly, one angel differs intelligibly from another.

Empirical differentiation is not in virtue of an ultimate intelligible difference; it is difference simply as a matter of fact. This pea is similar to that, but it is not the same as that; why not? It is simply a fact; there is not a reason.

Positively, empirical differentiation is in virtue of matter: matter is the unlimited passive potentiality of unintelligible difference; it explains why all the points in a line are each different from all the others. This is not quantity, for quantity adds continuity to this mere potentiality of difference: matter is the potentiality of difference as such.

4 Reality is either pure or impure.

Pure Reality is the aspect of the divine essence that is imitated or participated; it is necessarily intelligible in itself, for it is an aspect of the absolutely intelligible.

Impure reality is what must be besides this aspect as such for there to be more than the divine essence; thus, if the participated aspect is to be real, it cannot be a pure participation, for it necessarily is something that the Participated is not, viz., partial; similarly for imitation: the imitation cannot be the real original, else it would not be merely an imitation.

Impure reality is termed passive potency and pure reality act; hence, *actus limitatur per potentiam*.

Further, in God there is no potency; in all creatures there is potency; therefore, in all creatures there is something that there is not in God. Finally, both contingence and materiality are in themselves unintelligible; neither is found in God; both are found in all creatures in the world;

therefore, contingence and materiality are impure reality; also, as the real is positively real by participation or imitation of the Absolute, it remains that essence is the pure participation.

5 We draw two corollaries.
  (a) The reality of a thing is to be measured not by its existence nor by its particularity, if these are merely empirical, but by its measure of essence, of participation of the divine essence.
  (b) The lower grades of being are differentiated by affirmation and negation according to their measure of imitation: thus, existing but not living; living but not rational; rational but not immaterial.

This is the scope of differentiation by *esse absoluto*.

The same is true, possibly, of the differentiation of the angels.

In the Trinity, differentiation cannot be by the *esse absolutum* since each person is God exhaustively; hence it is by *esse relativum*, by the reality of opposed yet mutually implicit function.

6 Pure reality is dynamic.

God, whence all pure reality has its foundation, is a dynamic eternity of unlimited and immutable intellect and will; from this proceed all the attributes as well as the Persons; the attributes, for Wisdom is infinite intellect with infinite will; Goodness is infinite will with infinite intellect; omnipotence is the illimitation of will; immensity is the spiritual character of omnipotent will; etc., etc.

Physical reality, apart from its being a particular something, is, as the physicists tell us, energy; and a clear conception of the calculus is a great help to understanding the processions of St Thomas.

Biological reality, apart from its being particular somethings, is reproductive, self-adaptive, life.

The dynamism of reality is either *motus* or *energeia*.

Motus est actus entis in potentia inquantum huiusmodi.

Energeia est actus entis in actu inquantum huiusmodi (procession).

The dynamism of reality is somewhat obscured (ungroundedly) by the distinction between essence and nature. Essence is *quo quid est quod est*. Nature is the *principium intrinsecum actionis talis*. These two really coincide. To say that the essence of man is 'rational animal' is to think of man not in his absolute measure of reality but in his measure as a measure relative to that of animals. Man considered in himself is a particular conjunction of physical, organic, sensitive, and intellectual active potencies; abstract from the particularity and the contingent *suppositum* of the conjunction and we have the pure essence, a set of potencies. Now the actuation of these potencies does not regard man as such but man as existing and particular; hence the essence is merely the set of active potencies. But a nature is also a set of active potencies. Therefore, essence, considered absolutely, coincides with nature.

7   Individuation and Personality

Individuation is not the same as personality. An infant is actually individual but only potentially a personality. Formally, a personality is a combination of a habit of intellect and a habit of will, a particular mentality and character. This personality is constituted either by the Light and Charity that come of the Holy Ghost, and this gives the *anēr pneumatikos*; or in relation to the True, Good, and Beautiful, and this gives the *anēr psychikos*; or finally in relation to the sensible lower self of desire, and this gives the *anēr sarkikos*.

Hence it would seem that even among men personality is a relation; but it is a relation that arises from the spiritual potencies used well or abused and corresponds to the passive potency of individuation by matter, which supplies its initial possibility; we outgrow our individuation by matter, but we need it to begin with; further, we see the ground of immaterial existence in the intellectual and moral development of man.

5 A Theory of History[1]

1 Definition, material and formal objects

A theory of history is an explanatory account of those general forms of the movement of human history within which particular events take place.

It is concerned, then, not with the actors on the stage of time or how they play their parts but with that larger mold of time that sets the stage and calls the tune. More specifically it is concerned with the shifting of the stage and the change of tune, with the laws that govern the direction and content of historic movement through the past, in the present, and into the future.

Thus, theory of history differs from history as the universal, man, differs from its particular individuations, men. Not indeed that it is a study of the universal as such, the pure abstraction: its interest is, so to speak, the historic universal, human nature considered neither abstractly nor concretely, not apart from its individuations nor yet in its individuations but in the laws of its expansion through successive generations of new individuations.

There is another difference between theory of history and history. History is an empirical science and proceeds to theory, if at all, only from the

---

1 The comments of Michael Shute on this selection may be found in *Origins* at 110–20. Shute suggests 1937 as the year in which the selection was written. Lonergan's original manuscript is available in digital form on www.bernardlonergan.com at 71311DTE030.

facts. Theory of history, on the other hand, is an a priori construction; it deduces the forms of historical movement from the inherent laws of human nature; and it is an explanatory account of these laws in their origin, their efficacy, their combinations, their effects.

2 Procedure

A theory of history is necessarily a structure of many pieces: to orientate the reader from the start we offer an analogy of the procedure we shall follow in selecting our pieces and working them into a unity.

To understand the firing of a long-range gun, one would first distinguish the explanation of the initial and final explosions from the trajectory that joins them.

To understand the trajectory, there would first be called into consideration Newton's first law of motion, to the effect that a mass continues to move in a straight line with a constant velocity as long as other forces do not come into play.

The next step in the understanding of the trajectory would be to take into account the law of gravity; this gives the first approximation of the trajectory and bends Newton's straight line into a parabola.

The third step would be the more difficult calculation in which air resistance, wind, the movement of the earth are taken into account.

Of quite different character, on the other hand, is the explanation of the explosions, a matter of understanding the expansive nature of gas and its utilization to propel the projectile and ultimately disintegrate it.

Up to a certain point, this analogy holds with regard to the theory of history. For we distinguish the form from the content of historical movement. We arrive at an understanding of the form by laying down a general law and then correcting it in successive approximations. Having determined form, we turn to content, which is derived from other aspects of human nature. So much then for the parallel, which lies in the method of treatment. Where the parallel breaks down is that, while explosion and trajectory are two different things, with the understanding of one in no way dependent upon the understanding of the other, the form and the content of history are in reality one same thing and have as it were to be understood simultaneously to be understood at all. To revert to the example of the gun, we would have a more accurate analogy of our problem if the gun were loaded with a blank and the question were to determine the path of the exploding gas.

To offset this difficulty of the complexity of the matter, all that can be done is to supply the reader immediately with a synopsis of the argument, illustrate occasionally the exposition of the form of history by anticipating points from the exposition of the content, and suggest that to read the first part both before and after the second, though painfully tedious, might be helpful.

3 Scheme of exposition[2]

A The form of historical movement
   (a) The general law, the natural dialectic
   (b) The first correction, the dialectic of sin
   (c) The second correction, the supernatural dialectic
B The content of historical movement
   (a) The significance of human history
   (b) Ancient history
      (1) Natural dialectic, achievement of Near East
      (2) Dialectic of sin, paganism
      (3) Supernatural dialectic, Israel
   (c) Modern history
      (1) Natural dialectic, achievement of science
      (2) Dialectic of sin, Protestantism, liberalism, communism
      (3) Supernatural dialectic, Catholic Action

4 [A, (a)] The natural dialectic

The general law of the form of historical movement, the first and most remote approximation, is that this form is determined by the laws governing the development of human thought.

---

2 Shute writes, 'The document we now have contains all of section A, "The Form of Historical Movement." Section B, "The Content of Historical Movement," is missing except for part (a), "The Significance of Human History." This section functions as a prolegomenon to an actual consideration of the contents of history; the material that would have been derived from a consideration of the contents of historical movement either was never written or has been lost. In any case, it is clear that a consideration of the formal element constituted for Lonergan the fundamental concern.' Shute, *Origins* 112. In addition, we may add that some elements of the other matters contained in this outline may be found in the next three items.

To establish this law we have to show, *first*, that human action is governed by thought, *second*, that this thought tends to be uniform among contemporaries, *third*, what is the law of the historical development of thought.

First, then, action is governed by thought. This is manifest insofar as it means that a man cannot do what as a matter of fact he cannot think of doing; thus, an Eskimo cannot think of watering his camel because he has not one, nor of living on dates because date palms do not grow in his part of the world and he is unaware of their existence in other parts. However, it is our intention in asserting that action is governed by thought to lay down a principle not of absolute but of approximate truth. It is absolutely true that a man cannot do what he cannot think of doing; it is only approximately true that there is always something a man knows he ought to be doing and that man always does what he ought to do; yet that approximate truth is the first general law of history. It draws through time an ideal line, like Newton's constant velocity in a straight line; it has to be corrected by a law of gravitation; but the necessity of such correction does not invalidate the utility of a first approximation. On the other hand, the first part of our assertion, there is always something a man knows he ought to be doing, is almost accurately true. There are perplexities of the conscience, but the general obligations of life are plain, and they take up all our time. A man has to earn his living, and the way he ought to do that is the best way he can; he has domestic and civic and national and religious obligations, and these impose themselves; and such on the whole is the whole of human life.

Our second point was the tendency of human thought to be uniform among contemporaries. The proof of this is as follows. Men necessarily think in the same way if they have the same data before them in the same setting: for the act of understanding is determined by the phantasm; and the phantasm is determined by external experience. This is an absolute truth, and it yields a uniformity of thought not among all contemporaries but only among those whose experience coincides, among people of the same calling and the same district. Thus, the tendency to uniformity has to come from another factor, and this is the natural spread of ideas. An idea is never personal property: it will spontaneously propagate if its economic advantage is manifest; it will be deliberately propagated if it is to the advantage of parents or the state or religion; and if it is not propagated, then the theorist of history can disregard it.

Our third point was the law of the development of human thought, and here we have again to lay down a general law and then give a correction. The general law is that the intellect proceeds from the more general to the more particular. Understanding is at first of general principles and general applications, then of less general principles and more detailed applications, till finally the discriminations and discernment of intellect equal the complexity of a mass of concrete detail. A young man wishing to be an engineer has to begin with geometry and algebra and the calculus; has to potter in laboratories and hear lectures on atoms and draw pictures of tilted tetrahedrons as seen from different planes; only when he has been grounded in endless general principles will he be pronounced fit to erect a hotel or lay a drain. Rightly, because to understand the particular, man must first understand the general.

Now it is easy to see the correction needed to make this general law of the understanding a historical law of the understanding. When the prospective young engineer is learning factors and quadratic equations and that there is a logarithm to the square root of minus one, he is inclined to ask himself what this has to do with hotels and drains and the design of a faster aeroplane. Let us transpose this inclination from the tedium of study to the difficulty of discovery; think of a Greek who heard of Icarus and wished to build an aeroplane that was no myth; could he have thought of the necessity of first discovering higher mathematics and advanced physics?

It is true, then, that the understanding proceeds from the general to the particular; but it is also true that the understanding does not arrive at once at the right most general conceptions from which a complete understanding of the particular is possible. What happens is first the discovery of a general idea of little generality, which works itself out in applications as far as it will go. The limitations of this first idea become manifest in practice and lead to the discovery of a complementary opposed principle, an antithesis, which in turn is applied and extended; finally, from the simultaneous limitations of both ideas the intellect is led to discover a higher synthesis. Hence, some definitions.

A radical is in favor of the antithetical idea.

A conservative is afraid of the new higher synthesis.

A liberal wishes the new higher synthesis.

A compromise is an agreement to let thesis and antithesis both stand; it is imposed by the lack of the higher synthesis.

We turn to outlining the natural dialectic.

The data of experience determine thought; thought, in this first approximation, determines action; action creates the customs and institutions and objective social forms that constitute the data of experience, the routine of life.

If no new thought emerges in this circle, there is no history; for history is the history of change.

If new thought emerges, then it is some general idea that gradually discovers and applies its implications. This is the simple movement from the general idea to the particular acts of understanding dependent upon it. We term it an *expansion*.

The expansion works some transformation of the data through human action, makes more or less evident the insufficiency of its basic idea, [and] suggests a complementary antithetical idea. This antithesis has its expansion, reveals its insufficiency, and so to synthesis. But synthesis will not immediately be of sufficient generality, and so we have the process repeated, till the right most general ideas are discovered and their expansion creates another 'wonder of the world.'

Naturally enough, it is in the field of material development that instances are to be found of the workings of the natural dialectic. In building pyramids and palaces, men do what they ought to; and so the first law of history is not an approximation but almost absolutely true. The first law gives us the achievement of modern science; but we have now to consider a second law that explains why this achievement threatens to be a greater peril than a boon.

5 [A, (b)] The dialectic of sin

Sin is not doing what you know you ought to do. Thought dictates to action a course of life. Sin is action outside this ideal course.

This action, just as much as action dictated by thought, has its concrete effects in the external world and makes its contribution to that transformation of the data of experience which are the determinants of subsequent thought.

What the dialectic of sin is, is at once apparent. For as sin is wrong action, so it is a wrong transformation of the data of experience. And when the data are wrong, the act of understanding that will arise from the data will also necessarily be wrong.

Sin is a surd in the historical process. The right course of action is the understanding of the humanly unadulterated data. Sin, though it admits some explanation in human passion and frailty, is strictly an unintelligible: for it is going against the understanding, contradicting the intelligible; and what contradicts the intelligible is the unintelligible. Hence sin and its consequents have to be treated as surds in the data of experience;

to take them into account is to attempt the impossible; it is to attempt to understand the unintelligible.

But though it is to attempt the impossible, it does not follow that the attempt will not be made or that it will lack all color and plausibility. On the contrary, it is the truth that lacks plausibility in the face of the accumulated consequents of sin. It is the sins of men that create the divorce between theory and practice. What ought to be done is evident. But let us call it theory. Men act so differently. They lie and rob and even murder. They are haughtily indignant if accused. But must one not adopt their habits, if one is to succeed oneself? Be honest, but be realistic. Be careful, but do not pass up the main chance. Socrates teaching justice to Athens was an idle talker who had to be put out of the way; his insistence that pain was compatible with human happiness was but an arbitrary paradox to Aristotle.[3] The fact of sin by itself creates moral indifference in private life; it imposes *Realpolitik* in international relations; *impavidum ferient ruinae* was not said of the state.[4]

The spontaneous and immediate effect of accumulated sin in the data of experience is a distrust of the pure reason and abstract principles of conduct. This distrust is at once reasonable and unreasonable: *secundum quid* it is reasonable, for there is an objective foundation for it; *simpliciter* it is unreasonable, for that objective foundation is illusory, the consequent of sin, a surd to intellect, and so not to be taken into account in the proper operations of intellect. But the dialectic of sin consists not merely in this spontaneous and immediate effect; it is also the systematic corruption of the whole natural dialectic. For as the consequents of sin mingle inextricably with the consequents of right action in the data of experience, so these data suggest to undiscriminating intellects principles which are false yet accepted. Such general ideas have their expansions and call forth more violent antitheses; compromises succeed and then syntheses in which the whole of human life is placed upon a lower level. In modernism for the refined and communism for the downright our age seems to have arrived at the lowest of conceivable levels: the modernist makes of his intellect a toy to live according to his sentimental convictions; the communist denies all except the body and by combining violence with astuteness seeks to make the world conform to his materialistic conception of history.

3 See above, p. 14 and note 11, and below, p. 108 and note 23, and p. 171 and note 26.
4 Horace, *Odes*, Book III, Ode iii, line 8.

To contrast the natural dialectic with its corruption in the dialectic of sin, we may say that the natural dialectic is a series of ascending general principles each followed by expansion, antithesis, and a soluble problem, while the corrupted dialectic is a series of descending general principles each followed by an evil expansion, a violent antithesis, a really insoluble problem which nonetheless will appear to be solved by the negation of some truth and the consequent introduction of a still lower synthesis.

6 [A, (c)] The supernatural dialectic

The supernatural is either *quoad modum* or *quoad substantiam*: the supernatural is merely *quoad modum* if it merely transcends the actual potentialities of nature; it is *quoad substantiam* if it involves the introduction, into the historic flux, of God precisely as he is in himself, transcendent and absolute, mystery to the human intellect not because of unintelligibility but because of excess of intelligibility.

Thus, the supernatural dialectic is the contrary to the dialectic of sin. Both introduce what man cannot understand: but sin introduces what cannot be understood from lack of intelligibility; the supernatural introduces what cannot be understood from excess of intelligibility.

The law of the supernatural dialectic follows from its very nature: it transcends the human intellect and so must be simply conserved and not submitted to the play of thesis, antithesis, and higher synthesis which human intellect exerts upon its proper object.

But doing what ought not be done is a human weakness, so that the law of immutability which characterizes the supernatural is met by an antithesis in the dialectic of sin. This antithesis is rationalism: the attempt of man to understand what transcends the human intellect, an attempt which aggravates the evil and accelerates the downward course of the dialectic of sin. Without revealed religion to explain, modernism would be evident nonsense; without it to attack, communism would be stripped of its most virulent doctrines.

On the other hand, though the supernatural dialectic is exclusive of all evolution of doctrine, the very presence of its rationalist antithesis is the occasion for a development that lies in the express rejection of rationalist attacks and a consequent increase in the precision as well as an extension of the applications of the original deposit.

To enter into the positive aspects of the supernatural life lies outside the scope of this inquiry; we have only to point out a negative aspect, namely, that the supernatural is the restoration of nature in face of the dialectic of sin.

The dialectic of sin begins in rationalization of sin, in the view that sin is a fact which has to be taken into account, with its corollary that a sinful course of action in this world of sin is the only practical course of action. This the supernatural meets with a doctrine of the confession of sin: it obliges the sinner to admit he has done wrong, to admit that sin is sin, to be repented in the past and avoided in the future; this is to shift the opposition from the objective to the subjective field, to eliminate the objective antithesis of theory and practice, and substitute for it the recognition of a contradiction within the sinner, the contradiction between his conscience and his acts. It attacks the dialectic of sin at the root.

But the dialectic of sin is also theoretical error. And this the supernatural meets with the doctrine of faith. Sin leads to theoretical error because man would understand what is unintelligible. The doctrine of faith substitutes reason and will for understanding. You cannot understand how an infinitely good God could have created this world of pain: reason proves it, and the will quashes your sentimental difficulties. You cannot understand how Christ could be God and crucified: reason demonstrates the historical and philosophic *praeambula*; the will orders a supernatural act of faith based upon the unquestionable authority of God. There is no opposition between reason and faith: they are teammates. The whole opposition lies between the human understanding and faith: and that opposition irreducibly must remain because the data of experience are corrupted with the unintelligibility of sin while the object of faith is God in his transcendence, in the excess of intelligibility that is beyond the grasp of human understanding.

But man is not only reason; he is also passion, and that passion is inflamed beyond the restraint of reason in the vast cruelties of injustice and oppression when a man, a class, a nation rises in Achillean wrath to be revenged. The Old Testament tempered passion to justice; the New teaches charity. Love your enemies. Do good to them that hate you.

7 [B, (a)] The significance of human history

We have established three elements for a form of history; they are not yet the form, for they have to combine in the content to reveal their nature. We have now to study the content of history and at once approach its dominating element, the significance of history.

The question is, then, the meaning of these three elements: a natural dialectic representing the natural progress of man; a dialectic of sin breeding corruption; a supernatural dialectic working salvation. We inquire *first* the end of man, *second* the rationale of the existence of the dialectics, *third* the reason why they are what they are.

First, the end of man. Human nature is a universal: the intelligibility of all men is one intelligibility.

But the universal is individuated by matter, and the one intelligibility ceases to be one thing to become the intelligibility of many particulars. Now, when we say that the individuation is by matter, we mean that the individuation does not take place by the addition of an intelligible *differentia*, a specific difference; were that the case, the universal would cease, and we should have a number of particulars each to be understood in its own way. Material individuation is factual, empirical difference. The reason why this man is not that man is the same as the reason why this point of space is not that point: not an intelligible or specific difference but a mere matter of fact that is known as the fact of matter.

Now when a universal is individuated by matter, the finality may and normally does remain in the universal. Any species of animal is a universal individuated by matter: but the finality of any animal is the finality of the species as a whole, the good of the species which determines the natural laws of the species, and the good of man to whom the species is subordinated.

Further, the finality must remain in the universal, in the species as a whole, unless there arises the potentiality of intelligible difference in the materially individuated particulars. For finality is an aspect of the intelligibility of a thing; and if the intelligibility is universal, so the finality must be universal.

Now in man there does arise this potentiality of intelligible difference. *Homo est in genere intelligibilium ut potentia.*[5] He has intellect and will: the power of conceiving and of realizing intelligibilities. And because of this potential intelligible difference, the finality of man is not in the universal but in the particular with the potentiality.

What the finality is immediately follows. It is the realization of the potential intelligible difference. Man is individuated by matter that he may transcend matter by attaining intelligible differentiation. He succeeds

---

5 See Thomas Aquinas, *Summa theologiae*, 1, q. 87, a. 1.

by the intelligibility of his choices; he fails by the unintelligibility of his choices. His goal in either case lies beyond our vision: yet we may describe it as either the transcendence of the limitations of matter or a deeper intrusion into matter and its constraints.

Second, why should the dialectics exist? For it seems that they should not. For the finality of man is the finality of the particular. Yet the existence of the dialectics is a grave impediment to attaining the finality. For man attains by the intelligibility of his choices; the intelligibilities he has to choose are determined for him by the natural dialectic, while the dialectic of sin tends to make the unintelligible appear intelligible and vice versa; even the supernatural dialectic only mitigates and does not eliminate this evil.

The answer is not difficult. There is this solidarity of man in the attainment of individual finalities because natural laws follow the intelligible unit. The actual intelligible unit is the universal; actual laws of nature are therefore universal. The potential unit is the individual; in view of this potentiality the individual enjoys rights as an individual, though he must operate under universal conditions and within the limitations of universal laws.

This may appear an unsatisfactory solution. The end of the individual is everything to him. Why, then, should he be impeded in the attainment of his end by others who chose not intelligibly but unintelligibly? Why should every human sin accumulate in the objective field as an unintelligible datum to puzzle and mislead man, to tempt him and give him the excuse that doing wrong has some justification? So put, the difficulty reveals that it is *petitio principii*. For were the individual man unlimited by matter and under no obligations of solidarity with all other men with regard to his finality, then he would not be a material particular but would already be enjoying the status of an intelligible particular. Matter is not perfect individuation: it realizes the fact of individuality without conferring the rights of intelligible individuality.

Third, there is a further question. For the very nature of the natural dialectic is an apparent injustice. It is an antecedent law of sin before men actually commit sin. First, because the natural dialectic progresses from principles of low generality to principles of higher generality, it is inevitable that the men of the progress are mostly ignorant. To know the lower principle without knowing the higher is to have some direction, but an inadequate direction; it is in a way to be misdirected by persuasive half-truths. Second, this ignorance has its repercussions upon the soul of man; it involves a low activity of the higher faculties with a consequent overactivity of the lower faculties, with interest and desire centered in the field of sense, and because centered there necessarily and automatically exaggerated into concupiscence.

Still, this antecedent law, rather of occasions of sin than of sin itself, is only an apparent injustice. It is such because the occasions of sin, it might seem, should not come from nature. But it is only an apparent injustice, for the one thing that matters to the individual is his personal acts; if these are consciously sinful, he is damned, but not otherwise. *Per se* occasions of sin are no more than a gymnasium for virtue.

Nonetheless, there is a real law of sin, of which this law of the occasions of sin is an integral part.

For the natural scheme of humanity fits into a supernatural scheme. According to the supernatural scheme, as we know by revelation, humanity was created in the state of sanctifying grace, beloved by God with an infinite love that would produce man to the infinite goal of the beatific vision. This gratuitous love, to which corresponded the supernatural lovableness of grace in the soul of man, brought with it preternatural gifts of infused knowledge and freedom from concupiscence; and, as is plain, these preternatural gifts would have inverted the order of the natural dialectic, making it a direct expansion with deductive security instead of the antithetical expansion by inductive trial and error. Further, both grace and its gifts terminated in the universal, so that all nature was supernaturally elevated and the victory of Adam in his trial would have been the victory of all men. But Adam, and solidary with Adam humanity, sinned. Grace was lost, love forfeited, and by a natural consequence the preternatural gifts of infused understanding and freedom from concupiscence disappeared. Now sin is the absence of what could and should be present: actual sin is the absence in the sinner of the contrary act of good will; original sin is the absence in human nature of the supernatural grace that human nature in its solidarity had gratuitously received and maliciously lost; finally, the ignorance and moral difficulty that flow from the natural dialectic, that are vastly augmented by the sins of individuals in the course of history, constitute a law of sin in the sense that they proceed from sin both original and actual and lead to sin as direct occasions.

The first bestowal of grace upon humanity was an act of bounty; its second bestowal through Christ is, besides, an act of mercy. Christ, the beloved Son, 'in whom I am well pleased,' has grace in his own right; he is loved by God with an infinite love because he is himself God, coeternal

with the Father. The principle of the redemption is that those loved by
Christ are for Christ's sake loved by God with the love that is the infusion
of sanctifying grace and the indwelling of the Holy Spirit. Through the
love borne us by the humanity of Christ we are raised to the saving love
borne us by the divinity.

The economy of the redemption is the systematization of the principle
of the redemption in history. In this economy we may distinguish the
constitution of the redemption and its application.

The constitution of the redemption is the life and teaching and sacrificial death of Christ: this sacrificial death is at once the one act of the universe that can be of itself pleasing to God in that order of infinite pleasure
and love in which the supernatural moves; but besides being an act whose
finality is in God himself as infinite and transcendent, the sacrificial death
of Christ is also satisfaction for the sins of men, and merits for the sacred
humanity the right to unite to itself in its grace before God other men,
children of wrath and solidary with the sin of Adam.

The application of the redemption is the economy of the mystical body
of Christ.

Man is born solidary with Adam, both a sharer in Adam's sin and a
victim of the limitations of the natural dialectic and the perversions of the
dialectic of sin. The first point in the economy of the mystical body is its
constitution; man is solidary with Adam by carnal generation from Adam;
he becomes solidary with Christ by inclusion in the mystical body through
the sacrament of baptism. Thus Christ is a new Adam, the firstborn of
many in a new series of the universal, humanity; baptism is this regeneration, being born again of water and the Holy Ghost, into the new humanity which is Christ's and out of the old humanity which is the solidarity of
the descendants of Adam.

The second point in the economy of the mystical body is its character.
This character is putting off the old man and putting on the new, not
merely in the radical act of separation from Adam and union with Christ,
but in every act of life. It is conforming oneself to Christ, imitating Christ.
It is the transmission through time of the figure of Christ, to realize the
virtues of Christ in all the varieties of human life and circumstance. It
is passing the flaming torch of divine lovableness resplendent in Christ
as in its source into those nearer receptacles, the lives of holy men, that
everywhere the world may be luminous with the Light of the world and
everywhere sinful man may experience the drawing power of Christ on
his cross through the crucified lives of those who would sooner have to

suffer than be able to have pleasure because in suffering they come nearer to loving Christ as he ought to be loved.

The third point in the economy of the mystical body is its organization.
The mystical body of Christ is not an amorphous growth, nor does it
share the blind spontaneity that marks the unorganic. It is a true though
a spiritual society, with its hierarchy of members and functions, with its
teachers and magistrates, its doctrines, its laws, its sanctions. It is a reflex
society, the conscious preservation of the supernatural deposit of faith
against the usurpations of the natural dialectic, logically and deliberately
seeking consistency in all things with its basic principles and supernatural
foundation. And as a reflex society, the mystical body is the attainment
in humanity of what the natural dialectic should attain but fails to attain.

The fourth point in the economy of the mystical body is its force. To
produce a series of new Christs, children of Adam conformed to the Son
of God, is not the work of nature but of a supernatural power called
actual grace. In the illuminations and inspirations of the Holy Ghost lies
[sic] the wisdom of the saints and the balanced prudence of confessors,
the strength of martyrs and the purity of virgins. Thus, the Holy Ghost,
who formed the body of Christ in the womb of the Blessed Virgin, who
attracts men into the fold of the church, who guides them along the ways
of holiness within the church, is by a just analogy called the informing
soul of the mystical body; another aspect of this attribution to the Holy
Spirit lies in the infallibility guaranteed the supreme doctrinal and moral
direction of the church.

The fifth point in the economy of the mystical body is its finality, the
glory of God, pleasing God in the infinite order of the supernatural, and
by giving God such pleasure meriting eternal life, where in knowledge
of and union with the Infinite the supernatural reaches its term. As is
patent, to please God infinitely is not the work of man, to please God
supernaturally is not in the power of nature. Such pleasure comes from
Christ alone. But in giving it man may participate, above all, in the sacrifice of the mass, which is the repetition of the sacrifice of Calvary, but also
in every act that is done in Christ Jesus, in the mystical body of Christ,
by an organ or member of that body. Hence the insistence of St Paul in 1
Corinthians 13 upon the uselessness of what is without charity; hence also
the nature of merit, which is attached not to any human act but to acts
within the mystical body.

In conclusion, the significance of human history lies in all three elements of its form, in the supernatural element principally and per se, but

also in the natural element as giving the material basis and conditions of the supernatural element, and in the element of sin as in what calls forth from the mercy of God the restoration and salvation of what had been elevated and gone astray.

A more precise formulation of the significance of history would involve considerations of the content of history. This we would defer till we come to treat of Catholic Action, which is the role of the supernatural dialectic in the natural problems of human life.[6]

6 Shute, *Origins* 120: '... the manuscript ends here. A consideration of the scheme of exposition indicates that Lonergan intended to consider the operation of each of the three elements in terms of two historical stages, ancient and modern history, corresponding to the division of history into its pre-philosophic and philosophic phases.'

6 Outline of an Analytic Concept of History[1]

1 Analytic concepts

An analytic concept is knowing, and in some measure understanding, an object by analyzing it, not into genus and difference as in definition, but into its constitutive elements.

1 Michael Shute treats this and the next two documents in one section. His 'tentative assessment' (*Origins* 121) is that, while they were written around the same time (1937–38), the order of composition is probably the order in which they appear here. He regards the present document as 'clearly' earlier than the other two. It is also longer than either of the others (19 pages compared to 18 and 15 for the other two, respectively), despite the fact that it is incomplete. The initial outline indicates eight divisions, whereas the manuscript itself has only seven, with the seventh ('Renaissance') itself incomplete, suggesting perhaps that something has been lost. What we do have is written in essay form, whereas the next two texts are sketchy, though they do contain some developments on the present document. Shute comments, p. 121: 'In these documents

We give three examples of different types.

Metaphysics analytically conceives material reality as composed of existence and essence, accident and substance, matter and form.

Chemistry analytically conceives material substances as composed of other substances into which they may be resolved and from which they may be combined.

Mechanics analytically conceives, say, planetary motion as the resultant of a uniform velocity, an acceleration towards the sun, and minor accelerations towards the other planets.

The analytic concept of history, as we shall outline it,

(a) prescinding from accidental causes of history, such as plagues, and from the material factor in history, biology, (§ 2)

(b) attending to the essential cause of history, the action of human wills in the framework of solidarity, (§ 3)

(c) divides the totality of human acts into the three categories (§ 4) of acts according to nature, acts contrary to nature, acts above nature,

(d) analyzes the course of history as the resultant of an ideal line (§ 5) of progress from acts according to nature, of decline from acts (§ 6) contrary to nature, and of renaissance from the exercise of the supernatural virtues (§ 7),

(e) to view the whole as a multiple dialectic, a term we cannot explain in much less than all the pages that follow.[2]

What about free will? So far from belittling it, we make it the crux of the whole process. We outline history a priori by arguing, if all wills always act

---

Lonergan builds on the foundation worked out in TH ['A Theory of History']. He refines his formulation of the three moments of history, and he develops an explicit account of the three-stage division of history that compares to the formulation in his published work. There emerges explicitly the notion of the analytic conception of history and the concomitant refinement in his formulation of methodological procedures. Finally, Lonergan refines and generalizes his formulation of dialectic. It emerges as the unitive category for his analytic theory of history.' For further comments on all three documents, see ibid. 121–44.

Lonergan's original manuscript of the present essay is available in digital form on www.bernardlonergan.com at 71312DTE030.

2 In fact, the section on 'multiple dialectic' is not included in the manuscript that we have. Each of the next two documents, however, has a final section on this topic.

according to nature, this is the result, and in the proportion they act contrary to nature, that is the result, and, finally, in the measure that grace intervenes, decline recedes and progress is restored. This gives a view of history that leaves out '1066 and all that'[3] but is comparable to the pure mathematician's knowledge of planetary motion as a perturbed ellipse, *qua tale*. To discuss the value of such knowledge is outside our present scope.

2 *History*

We speak not of the history that is written (to it we shall refer as historiography) but the history that is written about.[4]

The material object of history is the aggregate of human actions, past, present, and future: every thought, word, and deed of every man.

The formal object of history (the aspect under which the material object is considered) differs, or at least diverges, according as one adopts the viewpoint of the historian or that of the theorist of history.

The historian is radically a chronicler; he would know matters of fact; he is as much concerned to determine, Who did it? as to narrate, What was done? And only tentatively and with misgivings will he venture from the solid routine of determining facts to the realm of causes.

The theorist of history is a scientist; first of all would he know causes; so he sets pure science before applied science, devoting his attention to what is essential and leaving the accidental to later developments of the pure theory; and because there is no science of the particular, he sets aside completely the question, Who did it? to consider solely, What was done?

We now attempt to define the formal object of theory of history.

---

3 The reference is to the book by W.C. Sellar and R.J. Yeatman, *1066 and All That: A Memorable History of England, Comprising All the Parts You Can Remember, Including 103 Good Things, 5 Bad Kings and 2 Genuine Dates*, illustrated by John Reynolds (London: Methuen & Co. Ltd, 1930). Lonergan's point, made humorously, is that the analytic concept of history does not address details.

Lonergan originally ended this sentence with 'as a perturbed ellipse and no further details.'

4 This distinction surfaces again many years later. See Bernard Lonergan, *Method in Theology*, vol. 14 in Collected Works of Bernard Lonergan, ed. Robert M. Doran and John D. Dadosky (Toronto: University of Toronto Press, 2017) 164.

In general, this formal object is human action in its causes. Such causes are many. There is the First Cause and secondary causes; among secondary causes, there are essential and accidental ones; among the essential may be distinguished those of formal and those of material import.

Human action as proceeding from the First Cause gives the formal object of a theological (natural or positive) theory of history. This science must follow and cannot precede philosophical theory of history, for in history the First Cause cooperates, and when causes cooperate we must begin not from the cause more excellent in itself but from the cause better known to us.

Human action as proceeding from secondary causes gives the formal object of philosophical theory of history. But here we must note that the term 'philosophical' must be used in a broad sense; we must take into account the supernatural virtues, which enter into the social order and have social effects of the greatest moment.

Among secondary causes we must distinguish accidental and essential. Accidental causes would be *actus hominis*[5] and such nonhuman events as plagues, famines, earthquakes, floods. Whatever their importance, be it great or small, they do not belong to pure theory. Give for instance as much importance as you please to the Black Death in English history: it remains that history is not essentially a succession of such events.

The essential cause of history is the human will – more accurately, human wills in the space-time framework of human solidarity. Of the many aspects under which the human will may be considered, we take two to make our point clear. The act of will may be considered in its native immanence as good or bad, meritorious or blameworthy: with that we are not immediately concerned. But the act of will, the human decision so to think or speak or act, has an effective transience; it influences both directly and indirectly other human decisions; and it is this solidarity of human decisions, this interdependence of the present and dependence of the present on the past, that would seem to constitute the essence of history. Proof we omit. Briefly, an event is 'historic' in the measure it influences human actions.[6]

---

5 Lonergan is referring to the distinction between an act of a human being that may have no moral significance (*actus hominis*) and an act of a human being that involves intellect and will (*actus humanus*). See Thomas Aquinas, *Summa theologiae*, 1–2, q. 1, a. 1.

6 The last sentence is handwritten in the margin. But see below, p. 158.

We spoke of decisions influencing other decisions both directly and indirectly: directly when, ready-made, they supply others with ways of thinking and acting, whether it be convincing of what is true, persuading to what is right, indoctrinating with falsehood, conspiring to evil, or, finally, adding to all these a judicious use of force; indirectly when decisions or aggregates of decisions create social situations which through reflection or by necessity favor or impose a type of mentality, a tendency of character, a course of action. Compare being born in Mayfair and in the jungle, for a representation and measure of this influence.

Finally, in the essential causes of history let us distinguish between those of material and those of formal moment: by formal we mean what determines, shapes; by material we mean what is determinable, what is not 'creative,' though it limits, handicaps, to a greater or less extent, the work of the formal, loosely 'creative' element. Now, both direct and indirect influence mentioned above are of formal import: they are in the historical process as determining factors. On the other hand, while procreation is an essential element in the history of man, it remains that biological laws or the relative excellence of races cannot be more than of material moment: race may or may not make it easier to think well and act properly; but such facility regards not the substance but the mode of acts, and however important de facto such facility might be, it cannot of its nature enter into the historic process as a determining element; it cannot, because its nature is to be determinable.

The formal object, then, of this attempt at theory of history is *the making and unmaking of man by man*. It sets aside all question of what person or what people did this or that, to concentrate on what is done. It prescinds from the accidental influence of 'acts of God' and *actus hominis*[,] as well as from the material factor of biology,[7] to consider mankind differentiated in its ways of living by diverse geographical environments, progressing with the expansion of natural powers, declining from the effects of sin, and knowing no renaissance save through the grace of God.

3 Human solidarity

Above we indicated reasons for regarding the solidarity of human decisions as the essence of history. We have here to state more precisely the

7 In the typescript Lonergan crossed out at this point the words 'if such exists.'

nature of this solidarity, for it is, as it were, the mechanism which compounds into a resultant the workings of nature, sin, and grace.

Solidarity has its radical or, if you will, substantial aspect, which is at the root of the accidental solidarity that more immediately concerns us. The radical solidarity of man is that he is a species, one nature, one intelligible, in many material individuations. This unity to speculative intellect, which abstracts from matter, would seem to set up an exigence, a law of nature, that man be treated as one. Matter individuates; it makes each man a distinct reality; but it does not make men distinct realities in the degree of independence in which angels are distinct. For matter individuates only to conjoin, to bind men together in the working out of their destiny. The angel is *in genere intelligibilium ut actus*; he is a world to himself. But man is *in genere intelligibilium ut potentia*;[8] and the actuation of that potency is not the work of individuals but of the species, with genius appearing at intervals not as the flowering of individuality but as the product of the age and the instrument of the race in its progress. Nor does the will, in this life, liberate the individual: at best the will follows the intellect. On the other hand, the individuation that matter gives has a teleology in its own line: it is the prerequisite of that development of personality, which if accidental is an intelligible individuation and would seem the ground (not the argument, perhaps) for a life beyond the grave in which, according to his merits, man lives either liberated from material conditions or hopelessly immersed in their routine.

We may point out that this view of radical solidarity affords the intellect some satisfaction not only with regard to the solidarity of human action but also with regard to our solidarity in Adam's sin and the solidarity of the mystical body of Christ.

The solidarity of human action may be summed up in the phrase: We make ourselves not out of ourselves but out of our environment.

We make ourselves, for the will is free. To the 'more or less' of all things finite it can oppose its absolute 'yes or no,' while the obscurities of this life make it regularly possible to apprehend some *ratio mali* in what is connected with the infinite Good.

We make ourselves, not out of ourselves. For our making of ourselves is motion and increment. *Quidquid movetur, ab alio movetur*.[9] *Nemo dat quod non*

---

8 See Thomas Aquinas, *Summa theologiae*, 1, q. 87, a. 1. See also below at note 20.

9 Thomas Aquinas, *Summa theologiae*, 1, q. 2, a. 3.

habet. Our minds are summations of impressions, apprehensions, more or less integrated by understanding; and such integration as we achieve is not our work but that of the *primum agens*, who presents the meaning of the universe and its parts to us by steps like a teacher of geometry in a school. Again, our virtue is acquired by many virtuous acts: but how do we perform the acts before we acquire the virtue yet to acquire it; there is the Great Artist, and the world's pedagogues are but his tools.

We make ourselves out of our environment. We would use the word 'environment' with some of the universality of the Ignatian *reliqua*.[10] There is the physical environment with all the influence that makes for geographical differentiations of men. There is the environment of family, where mutual love and confidence create a maximum of facility for mutual influence, while kinship readily sets up the embryonic state of tribe or clan with its sacrosanct traditions and customs.

Now consider a dilemma: either man remains in this loose organization and so remains to a great extent directly dependent on the bounty of nature (primitive hunters, fishers, fruit-gatherers) or he applies his intellect to the problem of existence, discovers agriculture and then the division of labor and the necessity of the state. This dilemma suggests a law, which we would put as follows.

First, any development of the 'higher culture' of arts and literature, science and philosophy, presupposes a measure of general security and leisure that can be attained only by an exploitation of discovery and invention in the economic field. What C[hristopher] Dawson calls the discovery of the ox made possible the higher culture for the few;[11] the modern discovery of the machine would seem to have its finality in making possible such culture to the many.

Second, the exploitation of discovery in the economic field brings in its train both specialization and organization: specialization, because the power of intellect is the power of the universal; organization, because specialization necessitates the ordering of society with different members attending to different ends and over these a hierarchy of others who attend to more general ends.

10 The reference is to the *Spiritual Exercises* of Ignatius Loyola, who in the 'Principle and Foundation' speaks of God's purpose in creating humankind, and then of the purpose of the 'other things on the face of the earth' (§ 23), the 'reliqua.' Lonergan's text has 'world environment,' The change from 'world' to 'word' is editorial. See below, p. 160.
11 See Dawson, *The Age of the Gods* 92–93.

Hence we may say that as matter individuates man without liberating him into full individuality, so the dependence of man upon the 'other' is in primitive society largely upon nature and to a small extent upon society, but, in proportion to human advance, this dependence shifts from dependence upon nature to an ever-increasing dependence upon society.

Our first point was the priority of economic development; our second that economic development liberates man from physical needs only to impose upon him social dependence. The third is that in proportion as economic development proceeds, the social unit is of necessity enlarged, because the greater the power of intellect, the higher the specialization and the broader the basis required.[12]

Now let us turn from this to the most fundamental point to be made in this section.

At all times there is some social organism, and in every organism there is a body of thought that is socially dominant and effective. The social organism, from the most primitive tribe to the world state, creates a channel of mutual influence: within this channel all men both tend to agree and, if they do not, are forced for the most part to act as though they did. The dominant thought is the socially effective thought; it goes into execution, while other thought, apart from minor manifestations in the present and a promise of change for the future, remains mere thought. Dominant thought, though it may change from year to year, still at each moment is the rule, the rule of action; other thought is the exception.

Now this dominant thought is subject to a dialectical process. Because it brings forth fruit in works, it concretely manifests its excellences and its shortcomings. Taking the matter more largely, we observe that the dominant thought at any time arose from the situation that preceded it; that its tendency is to transform the situation; that the transformed situation will give rise to new thought, and this not merely to suggest it but to impose it.

12 The words from 'because' to the end are handwritten after the following crossed out words: 'The temple states of Mesopotamia gave way to the ancient kingdoms; modern economic structure demands the substitution of some form of world state for our autonomous nations.'

By the dialectic, then, we mean the succession (within a social channel of mutual influence) of situation, thought, action, new situation, new thought, and so forth. Its principle is that as each individual forms his mind from the environment, so all individuals within an environment reflect the environment by their thought; from their thought proceed to action and the production of a new situation; which in its turn will be reflected by further thought and result in further action. We may note we are not concerned with the quality of the thought that arises from the situations: such thought may not arise at all, and then we have stagnation, as perhaps has been the even and dull tradition of China; such thought may be active yet increasingly wrong, and then the dialectic resembles the graph of oscillation in resonance; or it may be active and increasingly right, and then the dialectic resembles the graph of a damped oscillation.[13] But these points more in detail later.

Again, by the dialectic we do not mean Plato's orderly conversation, nor Hegel's expansion of concepts, nor Marx's fiction of an alternative to mechanical materialism. We mean something like an experiment, a process of trial and error; yet not a formal experiment such as is performed in a laboratory, for man is not so master of his fate; rather *an inverted experiment in which objective reality continuously strives to mold the mind of man into conformity with itself by revealing to man the evil arising from his errors.* We are familiar with the process by which experience and the lessons of life form the judgment and mind of the individual: project this process, *mutatis mutandis*, to the large-scale development which is the evolution of a social unit and you have an analogy to the dialectic.

Properly the dialectic belongs to the social unit. But ideas have no frontiers. The interaction of many dialectics we term the multiple dialectic. The two chief phenomena are transference and reaction. Transference may be temporal or spatial: temporal may be illustrated by the dependence of Greece on ancient Mesopotamia, of Europe on

---

13 Much has been made of Lonergan's comparison of the dialectic of history with the threefold approximation in Newton's planetary theory. See Lonergan's own acknowledgment of this comparison in Bernard Lonergan, '*Insight* Revisited,' in *A Second Collection*, vol. 13 in Collected Works of Bernard Lonergan, ed. Robert M. Doran and John D. Dadosky (Toronto: University of Toronto Press, 2016) 228; and see above, p. 83, and below, p. 106. But here, with oscillation graphs, we have another and, if anything, more complex comparison with notions developed in physics.

Rome; spatial by the repercussions of the French Revolution, by the two westernizations of Russia, by the modern development of Japan. Reaction is the control exercised by the native dialectic upon importations of ideas.

4 The analytic concept of history

In the last two sections we have argued that history, to the theorist of history, is essentially the multiple dialectic. It is by the analysis of the dialectic, then, that we may hope to arrive at the analytic concept of history. In this section we determine the three categories of the dialectic; in the following three we study their nature and interactions; in the last we indicate the broad lines of history as an application of the doctrine elaborated.[14]

Agere sequitur esse. But it is the peculiarity of man that his intellect must learn his nature and that his will is free to follow it. *Homologoumenōs tē phusei zēn* is not what must be but what ought to be. This gives immediately two categories of human actions: those according to nature and right reason; those contrary to nature and right reason.

We must observe that these two categories represent metaphysical ultimates. What is according to reason is intelligible: it belongs to a manifold of reality that fits together in harmony, not only in the external harmony of the rhythm of success and progress, but also in the higher and more important harmony of the intellect, which can apprehend in synthesis the many that in itself and in its relations is intelligible. (*Distinguish intelligible* in the sense of *knowable* and intelligible in the sense of *comprehensible*, understand-able [*sic*]: the former is the possible object of judgment, *est aut non est*; the latter is the possible object of intelligence, which in its first act asserts there is *why* and in its second act knows the *why*; the former is a larger category than the latter. We shall speak of the intelligible only in the latter sense.) Now what is contrary to right reason is in a strict sense unintelligible. To speak of explaining sin is, rigorously, nonsense: for sin is a desertion of intellect; it may have its pretenses, but it cannot have reasons that really are reasons, true reasons; for the truth of the matter is that it is against reason. Why did the angels sin? Why did Adam sin? There is no 'why.' We do not say that there is a reason why but that we cannot know it; we say there is no reason to be known. We do not deny

14 As was indicated earlier, this last section and part of the one preceding it seem to have been lost.

God had excellent reasons for permitting sin, though we do not grasp those reasons; hence we do not evacuate the *mysterium iniquitatis*. On the contrary, we add another, which however is not a mystery from excess of intelligibility but from lack of it.[15]

There is a third category of human actions: those above nature. Their intelligibility lies not in the natural order but [in] the supernatural. 'Those who are unspiritual do not receive the gifts of God's Spirit, for they are fool-ishness to them, and they are unable to understand them because they are spiritually discerned' (1 Corinthians 2.14).[16] We are owl-eyed in the day-light of the gods: that daylight is amidst us. 'The God who said, "Let light shine out of darkness" has shone in our hearts …' (see 2 Corinthians 4.6).[17]

Now as the first two categories are metaphysically ultimate, so also is the third. We deal with human actions as *intelligible to man*, as *unintelligible*, and as *too intelligible*. Beyond such a division the mind of man cannot go; there is no possible higher synthesis which could find an antithesis to the thesis of our analysis. There is not, because our analysis is framed on the frame that is the confines of our mind.

It is true that this analysis has the disadvantages of its generality: but *intellectus a magis generali ad magis particulare procedit*; so we do well to grasp at the beginning the most general. And further, we shall the more readily grasp the essential in historical situations by confining ourselves to what is most general.

We might finally observe that our analysis stands on the level of the Light-Darkness contrast in the New Testament: light – too intelligible; darkness – unintelligible.[18]

15 In the margin of this paragraph, a quotation from Augustine: 'Nemo ergo ex me scire quaerat, quod me nescire scio, nisi forte ut nescire discat, quod sciri non posse sciendum est.' *De civitate Dei* 12, 7: 'Let no one try to learn from me what I know I do not know; unless perhaps he learns not to know what should be known as something that cannot be known' (translation by Frederick E. Crowe in his edited version of Lonergan's 'Analytic Concept of History,' MƐTHOD: *Journal of Lonergan Studies* 11:1 [1993] 14 – see below, p. 154, note 1).

16 Lonergan cited this text in Latin: 'Animalis autem homo non percipit ea quae sunt Spiritus Dei: stultitia enim est illi, et non potest intelligere: quia spiritualiter examinatur.' The translation is taken from the New Revised Standard Version (NRSV).

17 Again, Lonergan cited this in Latin: 'Deus qui dixit de tenebris lucem splendescere, ipse illuxit in cordibus nostris.' And again the translation is that found in NRSV.

18 The material after the colon was added by hand in the manuscript.

5 *The ideal line*

An analogy will throw light on the issue. In mechanics the ideal line is drawn by Newton's First Law of Motion: that a body in motion and free from the influence of other forces continues indefinitely to move in a straight line and with uniform speed. No body ever so moved, not even for a mathematical instant; yet the law, so far from being untrue or useless, is the basis of classical mechanics. Similarly, we would draw an ideal line of history, establishing what would be the course of history under defined conditions, whether or not such conditions are or can be realized. This will give a first approximation to the actual course of history; in subsequent sections we hope to draw closer to the reality.[19]

We define the ideal line, then, as the course of history that would arise did man live according to his nature, did all men at all times in every thought, word, and deed obey the natural law.

The earthly task of man, the proximate end of his activity, is the making of man: giving him his body, the conditions of his life, the stuff from which he will perforce choose in the fashioning of his soul. Now it is in the nature of man that this task is not a routine, the unceasing repetition of identical products, but, as age succeeds age, a progress. *Homo est in genere intelligibilium ut potentia; procedit per actus incompletos ad actum perfectum.*[20] But this actuation of potency is not achieved in a lifetime; it can be the achievement only of the species, as each generation adds to the store of human attainment and education recapitulates in the young the intellectual evolution of the past.

Progress, so understood, is of the natural law. It is imposed with physical necessity by the natural law, for man will not resist its enticement. But it would seem imposed with moral necessity as well, at least if we understand this moral necessity to have its subject not in the individual but in the species, much as the obligation of propagating the race lies not upon men singly but [upon] all collectively. The reason would be that *potentia est propter actum*. The finality of man's capacities is their realization: to withdraw oneself from that finality would be to withdraw from life itself. A society that made its ideal to be traditional and self-perpetuating would be inert, for it neglects the greater good; fatalistic, for it is indifferent to

19 See above, note 13, and the reference given there.
20 Again, see Thomas Aquinas, *Summa theologiae*, 1, q. 87, a. 1; but add q. 85, a. 3.

the evils it suffers; insensitive, for it brings no remedy to suffering; psychologically such a society could not fail to be in decay; *le métier de l'homme est de se dépasser.*[21] On the other hand, the list of prohibitions demonstrated by moralists is but the necessary mode in which the substance of life, the realization of capacity, is achieved. The great precept is positive. The servant who wrapped his talent in a napkin was cast into exterior darkness; God gave the world to man with the command, 'Increase and fructify'; and the law of charity is the necessary disposition of the will if the intellect is to see things as they are; enlightened self-interest is a contradiction: for the self-seeker sees the world with a subjective bias that excludes enlightenment.

Since the instrument of progress is the intellect, it follows that the form of progress is a projection in history of the form of intellectual development. We outline the latter to determine the former.

The human intellect is a conscious potency conditioned by experience. Because it is conscious, it has two uses: one spontaneous; the other reflex. Because reflex use of intellect presupposes the erection of canons of thought and method, it follows that there is a spontaneous period that precedes a reflex period.

Again, because the intellect is conditioned by experience, we distinguish two fields in which it may operate. There is the philosophic field, which depends upon the mere fact of experience; and there is the scientific field, which depends upon the details of experience. Further, roughly corresponding to this difference of field of inquiry (which is the Scholastic distinction between *obiectum adaequatum et obiectum proportionatum*), there is a difference of intellectual operation. In the philosophic field, we reason; in the scientific field, we seek to understand. Not indeed that scientists do not reason, nor that philosophic synthesis is an anomaly; but that the great concern of the philosopher is to establish uncontrovertible truth,

21 Patrick Brown suggests in correspondence a possible source for this expression: 'There was a review by Joseph Ferchat of a book by Antonin Eymieu, *Le Gouvernement de soi-même*, vol. 3, *L'Art de vouloir* in the French Jesuit periodical *Études*, vol. 222 (January 1935) ... The review describes the "epilogue" of *L'Art de vouloir* as containing a dozen pages devoted to the development of the idea that *le métier de l'homme est de se dépasser.* And, indeed, that is both the title of Eymieu's epilogue and its basic theme ... Since Lonergan was in Amiens when he wrote "Analytic Concept" and its variations, it seems fairly plausible that he got the phrase either from the review by Joseph Ferchat or from the book by Antonin Eymieu.'

while that of the scientist is better and better to understand. (Hence, Belloc: Science as the enemy of truth.)[22]

The distinction between reason and understanding is apt to be perplexing. Let us illustrate from the *Gorgias*. Socrates demonstrates [that] justice [is] better than injustice; he appeals to reason; he insists that to sustain the contrary results necessarily in contradiction. But he cannot explain how it is so, how the slave who kills the tyrant and sets himself up in his place is not better but worse off for his injustice; he will invent a myth to satisfy understanding; but his real position is that 'how it is so, I do not know, that nonetheless I have met no one who could maintain the contrary and avoid contradiction' (509a).[23] (I trust I am not reading my meaning into the text.)

Now reason attains truth. Philosophy and mathematics have indeed their period of groping, but this lasts only till the most general term of the science is reached. After that, progress is not revolutionary but simply the achievement of greater accuracy and refinement. Aristotle was the first to discourse systematically on τὸ ὄν, and he remains the master of those who do so. The modern period of mathematics might seem to be opposed to our view: but rather perhaps confirms it, for the modern mathematician has been busy generalizing his concept of number, and with maximum generality attained, revolutionary progress becomes impossible.

On the other hand, the immediate goal of the understanding is to understand, to know the intelligibility of things. Now *per se intellectus est infallibilis*, so whenever we understand, necessarily per se we understand rightly. Still, the accidental is a regular occurrence. How is this? It is that our understanding is of the object as we apprehend it: let our apprehension be distorted or incomplete, then our understanding will indeed be true of what we apprehend yet not an attainment of the intelligibility of the object. Point out to a man who understands, but wrongly, the factor his view does not take into account; if you succeed in your effort he will say, 'I

22 Hilaire Belloc's essay 'Science as the Enemy of Truth' may be found online at: http://www.catholictradition.org/Classics/belloc2-7.htm; in print see chapter 10 in *Essays of a Catholic Layman in England* (London: Sheed & Ward, 1931), also published as *Essays of a Catholic* (New York: Macmillan, 1931/Charlotte, NC: Tan Books, 2009).

23 W.D. Woodhead's translation, in *The Collected Dialogues of Plato*, ed. Edith Hamilton and Huntington Cairns (Princeton: Princeton University Press, Bollingen Series LXXI, 1971) 291: 'I know not the truth in these affairs, but I do know that of all whom I have ever met either before or now no one who put forward another view has failed to appear ridiculous.'

never thought of that,' meaning that if the 'that' were not to be thought of, then his understanding would be right. Thus, even in correcting its errors the understanding witnesses to its per se infallibility.[24] We might note, then, that the significance of Newman's real apprehension as a criterion of certitude is that with real apprehension false understanding is impossible: real apprehension is exhaustive; granted an understanding of such apprehension there is the impossibility of any other factor or point of view being brought forward to require or effect a change of 'interpretation.'

The above outline of the nature of the understanding leads immediately to the outline of its progress: this is by thesis, antithesis, higher synthesis, in the sense that the understanding first integrates in an apperceptive unity a certain measure of fact, which gives the thesis, then discovers incompatible fact, which gives the antithesis, and finally forms the higher unity, the higher synthesis, which if not on the level of philosophic ultimates, is itself open to antithesis and still higher synthesis.

This progress of intellect through thesis, antithesis, and higher synthesis may be either purely intellectual or solidary with real progress. In the former case, it works itself out in the logical field or the laboratory. In the latter case, the thesis that is to find an antithesis is not so much wrong as incomplete: for were it simply wrong it could find its way into history only as the memory of a notorious failure. But without being wrong a thesis can be incomplete, as, for instance, classical education, which finds an antithesis in the 'modern side,' is certainly not simply wrong and arguably better than the modern side, yet in itself and in a new world incomplete.

So much, then, for the form of intellectual development. It falls into two periods, first a spontaneous use of intellect, then a reflex; and in both periods there are two fields of thought, with reason predominating in the one and understanding in the other. Now if we project this form of intellectual development upon the historical process, we obtain as the ideal line of history first a period of spontaneous history and then a period of reflex history.

24 Compare Lonergan in *Verbum*: 'No one misunderstands things as he imagines them: for insight into phantasm to be erroneous either one must fancy what is not or else fail to imagine what is; of itself, per se, apart from errors in imagining, insight is infallible; and, were that not so, one would not expect to correct misunderstandings by pointing out what has been overlooked or by correcting what mistakenly has been fancied.' Bernard Lonergan, *Verbum: Word and Idea in Aquinas*, vol. 2 in Collected Works of Bernard Lonergan, ed. Frederick E. Crowe and Robert M. Doran (Toronto: University of Toronto Press, 1997) 186.

The first subdivides into a period of spontaneous intellect and a period of reflex intellect. The second, though it enters the history of thought at the end of the first subdivision of the spontaneous period, becomes actual history only at the end of the second subdivision. In other words, between man's discovery of the reflex use of intellect and his utilization of this discovery for the systematic planning of the making of man by man, there is a period of real progress of reflex intellect within the framework of the spontaneous social unit of tribe or nation. But a diagram will make this clearer.

Spontaneous history:
Characteristic: social unit based on kinship, tribe, nation, race
A. Period of spontaneous intellect
Field of Reason: Popular religion and morality
Field of Understanding: Large-scale agriculture, mechanical arts
Economic and political structures
Fine arts, humanism, reflex intellect
B. Period of reflex intellect
Field of Reason: religion and morality on philosophic basis
Field of Understanding: Scientific method, applied science
Enlightenment
Theories of history

Reflex history:
Characteristic: subordination of spontaneous social units based on
    nation or race to world planning
Field of Reason: The 'general line' philosophically determined
Field of Understanding: Edification, from particular to general, of
    world state

We draw attention to the fact that we are dealing with the ideal line. Actual history is distorted by decline, while the supernatural even reverses the order of natural development: the church realized international society before progress had impressed upon man its importance and inevitability; philosophy preceded the fine arts in modern development.

6 Decline

We defined the ideal line as the consequent of integral and constant observance of the natural law. We now consider not a new and unrelated line but a deviation from the ideal, decline. It is defined as the consequent of violation of the natural law.

We distinguish three forms of decline: minor, major, compound. Minor is in the field of the understanding, the practical field. Major is in the field of the reason, the theoretical field.[25] Compound is the conjunction of the major and the minor.

The nature of minor decline seems to be as follows.

The new syntheses of progressive understanding have three disadvantages. It is not clear that they offer the 'better,' for practical questions are complex. It is certain that they threaten the liquidation of what is tried and established, and this is unwelcome to vested interests. In most cases they contain the element of risk and demand the spirit that contemns the sheltered life – insured from tip to toe – and so are met with the solid opposition of all whose wisdom rests on the base rock of stupidity. In consequence every little boy or girl is born conservative or liberal; there is social tension, for a thesis in company with antitheses sets up an objective exigence of advance; but what brings decline into the situation is the fact of sin.

Radix omnium malorum cupiditas.[26] As we have already pointed out, self-interest is not enlightened because it is not objective; it centers the world in the 'ego' of individual or class,[27] and neither is the center. This bias of practical thought transforms the distinction between those who govern and those who are governed into a distinction between the privileged and the depressed. Insensibly the privileged will find the solution to antitheses that affect themselves; too easily will they fail to acknowledge or pronounce insoluble the antitheses that militate against the well-being of the depressed. Thus they will enjoy a rapid expansion of progress, while the depressed by the mere fact of being left behind will become more and more depressed. But if the privileged are wise, they will not allow grievances to reach the magnitude that bursts into revolution; indeed, they generally have such wisdom, for the essence of the bourgeois soul is not at all cruelty nor vice but just the reinforcement of the instinct of self-preservation with a slight stupidity and a tepidity in enterprise;

---

25 Compare the minor and major surrenders of intelligence, *Insight* 255–57. On *Insight* see below, p. 156, note 5.

26 See 1 Timothy 6.10: 'For the love of money is a root of all kinds of evil' (NRSV).

27 We see in this paragraph early indications of what became in *Insight* the treatment of individual and group bias.

and revolutions have their causes mostly in the accidental field. Nonetheless, from the nature of the process we are describing, the yielding of the privileged cannot be outright; sets of palliatives will again and again be brought forward, and progress, if never too painfully, will ever be more and more complexly off the right track.

It is plain that the result is objective disorder: there is the fruit of rapid but narrow and unbalanced progress; there is the injustice of the existence of the depressed; there is the absurdity of the palliatives. And all, not merely abstract wrongs waiting on mere good will to be set right, but the concrete form of achievements, institutions, habits, customs, mentalities, characters. Further, this disorder is like the complex number; it contains the irrational. Sin is going against reason; it is in itself the unintelligible; its fruits partake its nature to objectify[28] and institutionalize and perpetuate the unintelligible. Progressive movement in the ideal line is from thesis through antithesis to higher synthesis; but to progress from an initial point of sinful disorder is quite a different thing, for the higher synthesis here cannot exist. The synthesis is an intelligible, and there is no intelligible synthesis that contains and embraces the unintelligible. Objective disorder sets problems that have no solution in the intellectual field. Acknowledge the *fait accompli* and you perpetuate injustice; refuse to acknowledge it and you are but fashioning an imaginary world in which you cannot live.

We may intercalate the observation that this accumulation of surds in the social situation and structure handicaps not progress itself but the progress of this or that people. The peoples fall by the wayside, but the transferences of the multiple dialectic pass the progress itself on for further increment to others. Of this more later.[29]

We may also note at once the error of both radicalism and realism. The radical attempts to impose an intellectual synthesis upon a situation that contains unintelligible elements: his idealism, with all its appeal to youth, is not wrong in itself; it is the world that is wrong; nonetheless, from that very wrongness of the world the radical also is wrong, for the intelligible does not embrace the unintelligible, the surd cannot be treated as an integer, and the radical is destined either to be Procrustean or [to] do nothing at all. On the other hand, the realist too is wrong; he is right in

28 The manuscript has 'objectivity.' The change is editorial.
29 Again, this 'more' does not appear in the manuscript that we now have. But it can be found at the end of the next two documents.

recognizing surds as surds; he is right insofar as it is choosing the less of two evils[30] in using the mere balancing of interests as a practical solution of a problem that has not in itself intelligibility; but the realist falls into error when he becomes realist not only about situations but also about men. To know men empirically is not to know them deeply: *agere sequitur esse* is not true of men as it is of things, because the actions of men are frequently contrary to their nature; so if the realist forms his idea of human nature from human action, his idea is false and its application disastrous – the disaster of *Realpolitik* and liberal economics.[31]

This brings us to major decline, decline in the philosophic field of religion and morality.

The essence of major decline is sin on principle. When men sin against their consciences, they do so as a last resort. When they deform their consciences, sin from being the exception becomes the law. It is this erection of sin into a law of action that constitutes the essence of major decline.

Its causes are manifold. There is the tendency to self-justification. The sinner hates his shame and his remorse and cuts the Gordian knot by denying sin to be sin. If he is isolated in his sin, this attempt meets with little success and gives little satisfaction. But if the sinners are many, then the inner lie becomes an outward lie; the liars reinforce one another in their affirmations and fling their doubting consciences aside as superstition, the dark fears that attack man when he is alone. A society in this state is avid of excitement, even if the excitement be only noise.

But this is not all. The lie of self-justification is not without its show of argument, for in the objective situation there stands the unintelligible, the surd produced by sin, which enters thought as a datum so that self-justification appears to have objectivity and truth. 'Business is business.' You say that that is immoral. But what else can business be?

In the third place, there is the general discredit of reason.[32] Philosophers can demonstrate what should be, but their adamantine laws are sheer naiveté ('it seems so evident'), their vision of the infinite Good too much out of harmony with this sad world to be true. Philosophy takes on the soberer task of determining why philosophers are wrong, and mankind becomes a derelict ship, its rudder broken.

30 The words from 'insofar' are added by hand in the margin.
31 On liberal economics, see below, p. 172.
32 Handwritten above 'of reason': 'cf. Socrates at Athens.'

There rise the winds of doctrine. The place vacated by reason and philosophy is filled by the understanding, fashioning *Weltanshauungen*, making thought a Babel, and giving every monomania the chance to become a sect.

But insensibly we have slipped from the causes into the course of the major decline. Let us go back to treat this with slightly greater fullness.

Logically the whole of the major decline is contained in its first step. To sin is to repudiate reason, to cancel what is highest in man and unchain an animal, with intellect the slave of instinct and passion. *At nemo repente summus*. Men live not by reasoning but by judging; they change not at a stroke but by degrees. There seem three elements in the course of the major decline.

First, there is the gradual deformation of conscience. One by one and each by stages, sins pass from being exceptions to being rules, till the critical stage is reached and decline itself becomes a principle with the assertion that morality can be revised.

Second, there is the series of lower syntheses in the field of reason now invaded by the understanding. Sin is social evil. The common good requires that at each instant as much as possible of a fading ideal be preserved. It is a losing game, but it is played in all seriousness. First, God is called out of mystery to be made the immanent sanction of social well-being, the totem of the hunters, the sky-god of the nomads, the Great Mother of the agriculturalists, the household gods of marriage. But what proceeded from unity to multiplicity next passes from being good to being evil; and what began as the sanction of morality ends as a provocation to depravity. Or to take the example from the reflex period, our own, there is first Catholicism, then Christianity, then reason, then naturalism, and finally – *nihil sanctum* – any of the systems whose premise is not man as he ought to be but man as he actually is, the radical acceptance of realism.

Third, each of the stages in the succession of lower syntheses calls forth a human mysticism: an appeal to all in man except his reason, to tradition, to glory, to ambition, to pride, to dreams, and to emotions. The mysticism is the organized lie of a society, defending what it was and, for the moment, preventing it from being worse than it will be. Thus we have the mysticisms of Protestantism and the nation, the mysticism of rationalism and free-masonry, the mysticism of naturalism and progress, the mysticism of the revolution in Russia, the race in Germany, traditional glory in Italy.

It is the nature of the human mysticism to be a drug; it is administered to the unhealthy in the hope of averting the catastrophe of death; it produces the semblance and effects of vitality for a time; it has a low efficiency, achieving ordinary living only in the tense atmosphere of wartime. As drugs differ in potency, so do mysticisms. Protestantism based itself on the mysticism of righteousness; National Socialism on the mysticism of race; Communism on the mysticism of revolution: as each of these falls short of a whole view of human nature, in that measure it is a lie and its mysticism drug-like in its effects.

So much for major decline, which terminates in the emancipation of man from reason and *his enslavement to the accidental causes of history*. We have now to consider compound decline, the interactions of the major and minor declines.

The major decline hastens the minor. Man achieves at once without revolutionary progress the truths of the field of reason; he needs this to give the progress of the understanding its directives. The effect of the major decline upon the minor is that progress is robbed of its compass. This might be thought a little thing: a principle is so small compared to a skyscraper; what can it matter in a city, a nation, the world? But every error when put in practice is an evil, and the magnitude of the evil may be measured by the generality of the erroneous principle: an error in the thousands is a thousand times worse than an error in the units; an error in the plan is the ruin of a construction; and error in principle is the ruin of all constructions. But the insidiousness of the major decline is that the errors it fosters are not in the field of science, if you except the human sciences, but in the whole orientation of science and its applications. Things are well made but for the wrong ends. Chemistry continues to advance – more and more for the making of better and better bombs. Biology extends its field – and the extension is captured to give the prestige of science to the naturalist mysticism. Economics is discovered – to create the modern agony by its false realism.

Alone, the minor decline results in disorder. Accelerated and complicated by major decline, the minor rushes towards chaos. And at each moment on the way, the major is itself in turn accelerated, for it is the minor that supplies the objective unintelligibility that more and more discredits truth and justice.

On the other hand, the minor decline has its proper contribution to the major. We have spoken of the successive lower syntheses with their complementary mysticisms that characterize the major decline. The mechanism for their imposition, for the inflammation of passion that destroys the old view and heralds the new as salvation, is the revolutionary tendency inherent in the injustice and tension of the minor decline. Rome is corrupt, and the princes revolt and impose national churches. The monarchy is corrupt, and the bourgeois revolt to establish the lay state. The bourgeois are corrupt, and the people revolt, anti-God, for religion that did not control the state, that did not prevent their exploitation, is not truth but an opiate merely to soothe the revolutionary nerve.

We do not wish to imply that every revolution is necessarily for the worse, for we speak of the successive revolutions of decline, and find our typical examples in the Protestant, the French, and the Russian. On the other hand, the violent revolution is by no means essential to decline: if there is little regret for the ideal that is being lost, then the left wing of one generation may easily be the right of the next, and this process of revolution within the constitution attains its maximum velocity when the policy of the right is more prudently to execute the policy of the harum-scarums on the left. Finally, we may observe that among the revolutions of decline are to be counted not only civil strife, for injustice is international as well as national, but also the rising of a whole people against the wrong, real or fancied, done them by the world.

What are the terminal phenomena of decline? First, there is the objective and unintelligible chaos, the accumulated product of sin. Second, there is the bankruptcy of intellect – truth a question mark and morality a convention – with the consequent atomization of society and the pullulation of superstitious sects. Third, there is *taedium vitae*, for unless man has something he will die for, he cannot live.

The multiple dialectic, taking the form of a struggle between nations, delays this end long after reason has been completely ruled out of court. The nation is a spontaneous social unit, for we can trust those who speak and therefore think as we do on every little thing, we cannot but feel misgiving in dealing with those whose language and mental atmosphere is different from our own, and the legend of common blood confirmed by the common characteristics of inbreeding supplies an easy mysticism. The nation, then, is the beast that will make intellect its slave when reason is dethroned. It will survive as long as there are wars to fight: *tamquam pupillis civibus tutorem videns necessarium esse terrorem*,[33] in Augustine's

33 'a wholesome fear would be a fit guardian for the citizens' (Augustine, *De civitate Dei*, I, 30).

presentation of Scipio's *Carthago non delenda*. Will one eventually rise to empire that it may decay of gluttony and lust, as ancient Rome? Or will the mutual thrust of too-sharp swords kill simultaneously all? With the complete dethronement of reason, we are out of essential history. The question does not concern us.

7 Renaissance

Progress is the thesis of nature; decline the antithesis of sin; to find the higher synthesis to these two we must raise our eyes over the horizon of this world. It is not the mind of man that can make issue with the unintelligibility of sin: yet the mind of man is the highest in man, and by decline man has forfeited even that.

Renaissance, then, can be no routine spring, the coming to life of what was dead as a mere matter of course. There must emerge within the confines of humanity a new and higher order, and into that order, renouncing his old self, must man ascend. The Trotskyist doctrine of 'continuous revolution' is meaningless on the level of man: for though it have its palpable premise in the surds of the social situation, surds never completely eliminated, it can have no realization there.[34] For the 'revolution' to succeed, capturing a society, is its betrayal: for if it holds its prey, it stabilizes itself in the old frame with bureaucrats supplanting bourgeois; and if it lets its prey go, then what has it done? The real truth of the continuous revolution can be found only on a higher level, the level of a self-renunciation that is a new birth into a higher order.

What is the higher order?

It is the emergence in man of what transcends man as man transcends[35] the beast, the beast the plant, plants the physical elements.[36] From this definition we may deduce the four characteristics of the higher order, the four columns of a new 'higher criticism' to replace the Hegelian.

---

34 Leon Trotsky, *The Permanent Revolution* (New York: Pioneer Publishers, 1931). See pp. 147 and 173 below. And see also Bernard Lonergan, 'Secondary Patrons of Canada, ' in *Shorter Papers*, vol. 20 in Collected Works of Bernard Lonergan, ed. Robert C. Croken, Robert M. Doran, and H. Daniel Monsour (Toronto: University of Toronto Press, 2007) 66 and note 6.

35 The word 'transcends' is an editorial addition.

36 See below, p. 147 and note 20.

First, the new order transcends man: therefore, it would be to his understanding mystery, for it would be to his understanding what the understanding of man is to the brute.

Second, the new order would be knowable: man knows being, and outside being there is nothing; man then could conceive the new order as real and transcending; his knowledge of it would be analogous to the scientist's knowledge of empirical law, for the scientist knows that light refracts and does not understand precisely why; that is the similarity of the analogy; the difference is that the scientist could know why light refracts but man could not know the 'why,' the *ratio intelligibilis*, of the new order.

Third, man would not be able of himself to raise himself into the new order: for the new order would be transcendent, and nothing can transcend itself.

Fourth, man in the new order would not have his nature negated but included in a higher synthesis: as man transcends but does not negate what is below him – as a mass of matter, he is under the laws of mechanics; as alive, he is under the law of cellular development and decay; as sentient, he has the perceptions and appetites of the brute – so in the higher order, the laws of the nature of man remain, though embraced in a higher synthesis. Hence the new order would be to man: individualist, rational, obligatory, mystical, social, authoritarian.

It would be individualist, for man in his finality is motion from material to intelligible individuation, the individuation of personality.

It would be rational: *quidquid recipitur ad modum recipientis recipitur*; man is rational by nature; therefore, his movement into the new order would be a rational act on his part. Corollary: for the acceptance of the transcendent to be rational, there must be evidence of its transcendence; i.e., miracles.

It would be obligatory: man must follow reason, must accept the truth reason demonstrates.

It would be mystical, i.e., have an integral appeal to man: for reason is but part of man, and not the part that moves for the most part.

It would be social, for man is of his nature social, works out his destiny collectively, makes himself only out of an environment.

It would be authoritarian: for what is transcendent, obligatory, mystical, and social is authoritarian.

So much for an indication of the basic characteristics of the new order. We turn to such as concern history.

In the first place, no theory of history that does not envisage the emergence in humanity of the transcendent can embrace the facts of the new order. Thus, Hegelian and rationalist higher criticism has been engaged in the essentially futile and nonsensible task of explaining away the facts of the New Testament and Old Testament: theory is to explain, not to explain away; it is to account for the fact, not to show that the fact could not arise.

In the second place, because the new order is a higher synthesis of the actual order of progress and decline, it will of its nature dissolve decline and reestablish progress. By reason and intelligence man is better off as an animal than the animal can be. Similarly, seek ye first the kingdom of God and all these things shall be added you [Matthew 6.33].

Now to meet major decline the new order must meet and counteract its three causes: self-justification, the accumulation of surds in the objective social situation, the discrediting of reason.

Hence, to meet self-justification the new order must teach penance. Self-justification, the pretense that sin is not sin, is the alternative to man's frankly admitting that he has sinned and his resolving not to sin again. Thus, movement into the new order should have the character of liberation from sin; while relapse into sin should be a deprivation of the higher life.

Next, to eliminate the surds of the social situation the new order should teach a virtue that goes beyond justice. Justice evenhandedly perpetuates the evil that has been done. To remove that evil, to provide a fresh start to humanity, there is required charity. Thus, the new order must be instinct with love, a brotherhood that is a reality and not a mere high-sounding pretense, that proves itself not by professions of friendliness but by deeds of self-sacrifice.

Third, to prevent the discrediting of reason, the new order should habituate man to hold the balance between reason and understanding. This it will do, for it requires faith, the assent to mystery (to what cannot be understood by man because it transcends him) because of rational demonstration.

Penance, charity, faith: these three strike at the roots of major decline.

The new order must also meet minor decline. Man is ever prone to sin, so it must bear startling witness to the possibility of man's overcoming temptation. The world of sense is ever deluding man into egoism, so it must bear witness within the world of sense to the renunciation of self that the new order demands. Man does less than he should: the full flowering of the new order would do more, and that precisely along the lines that make for minor decline.

Radix omnium malorum cupiditas. The new order will invite man to a complete renunciation of property.

It is the beast that blinds man to decline and makes him indifferent to its effects. The new order will invite men to a complete renunciation of the pleasures of the flesh.

It is the revolutionary spirit that transforms tension into rage to tear down what was better and set up and enforce, in hymns of hate, what is worse. The new order will invite men to form model societies in which the individual wills only to obey.

The spirit of poverty, chastity, and obedience would exorcise minor decline. That the spirit may actually exist, an elite must observe the letter, living not on the level of this world but, though still in the world, on the level of the new order.

Confronting decline, the new order would reestablish progress.

The condition of progress is ordered freedom. Freedom, for only the free play and interplay of all intelligences, each working on the concrete problems immediately confronting it, can discover the endless nuances of that 'better' which it is the work of progress at each moment to attain. Freedom, again because only the individual can afford to take the risks involved in the continuous trial and error of advance. Freedom, finally, because it is the nature of man to be free, and to interfere with the inner harmony and ease of his spirit is to kill the goose that lays the golden eggs. Yet ordered freedom. First, the order of the proper balance between reason and understanding: reason determines for all time the 'general line' of human life, the conditions that must be observed under any circumstances if life is to be lived. Second, the order of the will that follows the intellect, that allows the dispassionate and absolute-centered intellect to guide, that does not revolt to the disorder of egoism, class spirit, nationalism. And finally, not only ordered freedom but free order: the order must be not merely accepted but positively willed by each individual; it is not to be imposed from without, for such imposition is radically ineffective; of its nature it must spring from the *autoliberazione* of the self-renouncing will. True, there must be at any time in any human society the 'forces' of law and order: but these forces must be reduced to the minimum and not made the principle of social order; they must exist not to provide the rule but to take care of the exceptions; and in fact they can take care only of the exceptions: you cannot indict a whole nation.

The new order fulfills this condition of progress, not merely by confronting decline, but by inspiring man. Simply because the transcendent has been given to man, he is reconciled to his God, to nature, to his lot. The joy of hope, the vision that all things are good indeed, is restored. Manfully he sets himself to the task of the making of man.

The new order exists. It has given the world its credentials. It is divine. The transcendent that has emerged in humanity is God, the Word made flesh; and he has assumed our nature, that we may participate in his. Now the appearance of the Word in the world places the world in a cosmic perspective that reaches to the infinite majesty of God to reveal in blinding light two truths that must be grasped if the thought of the historical process is not to be a nightmare. The first is that the good deeds of man are, as man himself, infinitesimals: the work of an unneeded servant. The second is that the sins of man are not merely violations of natural law, not merely the corruption of humanity, but offenses against God himself. *Delicta quis intelliget?* None of us, to be sure, but the more we approach to some inkling of an understanding of the gravity of sin, the greater the possibility of our seeing things as they are. The history of man is the monotonous story of the reign of sin; the wages of sin is death, death of the soul, death of the body, death to every ideal and dream and hope. The economy of the new order is *per mortem ad vitam*; the higher synthesis does not negate the law of death pronounced by sin; but it does make death fruitful. And the fountainhead of that fruitfulness is the Word who took upon himself a human nature not to negate the law of death but to die sacrificially in reparation for the sins of mankind. He who stood in the waters of the Jordan to hear the Father say, 'This is my beloved Son in whom I am well pleased,' is also the eternal Priest and Victim that through him the Father may look upon men made solidary with him, baptized in his death (Romans 6), communicating in the body given over for us, and by that look transform them into children of God: *amicus amat amicos amici.* That is the supreme moment of history, and all the rest its diluted epiphany. The world is an altar; mankind the victim; the question whether man will offer the sacrifice of himself in reparation for sin or rebel not only to no purpose but without any ground. For that the world is an altar, life a cross, and death its goal, is not of God but of man; man has sinned and must die; but the good news to men of good will is that their death, if it be in the Lord, is birth into the life of God.

'But if Christ is in you, though the body is dead because of sin, the Spirit is life because of righteousness' (Romans 8.10).[37] But the body is not at once a corpse, not at once sown in corruption to rise in glory. The new order has its expansion within the old, the edification of the space-time complement of Christ, his mystical body, which we have now to consider in its inner law, in its relation with the world, in its accidental progress and partial declines.

In its inner law, the mystical body presents three aspects. First, there is the historical premotion of the individual from Christ.[38] Second, there is the assimilation of the individual to Christ by the Spirit of Christ. Third, there is the sacramental union of the individual with Christ and the whole mystical body.

As to the first, in forming and sending his apostles to teach all men, promising them to be with them all days to the consummation of the world, our Lord initiated a historical movement, founded a church to instruct and shepherd, bind and loose, the men of good will who would hear them as him. This action creates a new element in human environment, a set of premotions of spiritual significance in addition to the premotions of the geographical and politico-social environments spoken of above (§ 3). Man makes himself out of his environment: the church is Christ perpetuating himself historically, placing himself in the environment as the material from which we may make ourselves. Hence the significance of Christian solitude and meditation, the systematic effort to cut off other premotions and grow on premotions from Christ.

As to the second, Christ not only founded a church but sent the Holy Spirit. The Holy Spirit, the Spirit of Christ, assimilates to Christ. First radically, as Christ is substantially sanctified by the hypostatic union, so those born of the Spirit are accidentally sanctified by grace, a participation of what is divine in its divinity (*analogice divinum qua divinum*). Second

37 Lonergan here quoted the Greek, probably from memory, since his quotation is not quite exact.

38 Handwritten at this point above 'from Christ': '*fides ex auditu*' (faith is from hearing). The question of the historical causality of Christ remained with Lonergan and was addressed perhaps most fully in the final chapter of the manuscript that he wrote on redemption, probably in 1958, that now constitutes the second part of volume 9 in his Collected Works, *The Redemption*, trans. Michael G. Shields, ed. Robert M. Doran, H. Daniel Monsour, and Jeremy D. Wilkins (Toronto: University of Toronto Press, 2018).

dynamically, as the humanity of Christ is the perfect expression in nature of grace, so the action of the Spirit tends in each individual to express grace in nature and so make other Christs. Hence the imitation not only of Christ but also of the saints, those accredited by the church to say with St Paul, 'Be ye imitators of me as I am of Christ' [1 Corinthians 11.1]. Thus, all Christian holiness is an enrichment and intensification and renewal of the specifically Christian environment or set of premotions. On the other hand, the ideal of the religious who vows obedience is that by his vow he places his acts under a special providence that in all things he may do the will of God, thus raising himself above the life of self-interest and the life of natural intellect and will to the level of the action of the Spirit.

This complex interdependence, both inner and outer, of the members of the mystical body among themselves and their dependence through the Spirit on Christ reaches its culmination in sacramental union. In the mass, the sacrifice of Christ is reconstituted, and the Christian offers as an oblation in the odor of sweetness to God both the offering of Christ and its complement, the offering of his daily mortification and eventual death. The Christian thus participates [in] the supreme act of Christ and partakes in the supreme act of history. His participation in the act is consummated in communion, partaking in love and thanksgiving the body given over for us, the blood shed for us, to be one in him as he is one in the Father.

Our next topic was the relation between the mystical body and the world. To the mystical body the world is the matter it would embrace, inform, integrate into itself. The mission of the apostles is to all nations, the prayer commanded by St Paul is for all men. On the other hand, the attitude of the world to the mystical body is one of utter incomprehension: the mystical body asserts the supra-intelligible, but the world necessarily judges by its own standards. At best these are insufficient, and though a passing mood of enlightenment may for a few centuries urge tolerance and the open mind, in the long run the world must be hostile. The Christian transcendence of this life is inevitably taken as *odium humani generis*; hate breeds hate, and the seeming hate of the Christian calls forth the *odium fidei*. '*Christiani ad leones*' was not an imperial order but a popular cry; '*pluvia defit, causa Christiani*' expresses a quieter mood of the same mentality.

Yet *sanguis martyrum, semen ecclesiae*. We are baptized in the death of Christ (Romans 6); but we bring others to baptism by shedding our own blood. It is the supreme law of the economy of grace: *per mortem ad vitam*.

'For while we live, we are always being given up to death for Jesus' sake, so that the life of Jesus may be made visible in our mortal flesh. So death is at work in us, but life in you' (2 Corinthians 4.11–12).[39] Martyrdom is the supreme assimilation to Christ, the moment when Christ shines most radiantly in the *alter Christus*, as it is also the moment when in the persecutor the *deboire* of a violent act not consummated sets in. But much more than any such psychological mechanism is the resonance in high heaven of the martyr's sacrifice, his completion of what is lacking in the sufferings of Christ.

More generally, it is not only that the church cannot fail but that her failures are triumphs, her disasters victories. Persecution is the knife with which the heavenly gardener lops off the dead branches and prunes the living to bring forth heroic fruit. The kingdom of heaven is not in word but in power. Yet it is not ours to decide whether we labor in mere words or in power. The whole of tradition teaches us to make the best use of the natural means at our disposal, and all we can do is make that best use, convinced of its inefficacy, and praying for the grace that includes many others and is the shortcut to perfection, the grace of a lot of suffering. We are not the vine, much less the gardener, but only the branches to be pruned if good and cut away if faithless.

The operation of the mystical body is not only on the supernatural level but also on the natural. The latter now concerns us. We consider it first in its partial declines and then in its progress.

First, there is minor decline. We have argued that the observance of the counsels by an elite is the immediate and practical salt of the earth. To observe the natural law without grace is an impossibility. To be assured that with grace that observance is possible, man needs before his eyes the actual accomplishment of more; while to be guided in his judgments, general and particular, moral and practical, man must have in his midst the influence of a wisdom that is unclouded by the miasma of the world, that comes of the sustained effort of prayer, seeing God in all things. If then the salt lose its savor, if the light of the world be dimmed, all is lost. The counsels are denounced as a fraud because those who profess to follow them are found wanting; and with the counsels gone and the world's

---

39 Lonergan cited this text in Latin: 'Semper enim nos qui vivimus in mortem tradimur propter Iesum ut et vita Iesu manifestetur in carne nostra mortali: unde mors in nobis operatur, vita autem in vobis.' The translation is that found in NRSV.

teachers discredited, the commandments and the faith are in jeopardy. Minor decline has begun, and the door opened to major.

Nor is minor decline in the church without its mechanism. As believer to unbeliever seems guilty of an *odium humani generis*, so within the mystical body there is a similar tension between those who in varying degrees would make the best of both worlds and those who strive for the full flowering of grace in nature. The lives of the saints are perplexing; their presence is annoying. For the saints are signs of contradiction, dividing those about them into hero worshippers and persecutors: the former bear testimony to their virtue; the latter augment it, providing the saints with their trials. This tension then creates a spirit of hostility that can criticize even what is perfect. But when those who profess to follow the counsels stain their profession with human incompetence and bungling, there is anticlericalism; when they fall from their ideals, there is open rebellion.

Major decline is excluded from the church by providential guidance. Thus the possibility of major decline in Christianity is schism; its actuality is heresy. The schismatic rejects spiritual authority because it conflicts with his interests or hurts his pride: and he may justify his sin by appealing to the objective unintelligible of minor decline in the church. The heretic, on the other hand, represents the revolt of the understanding against the transcendence of Christian doctrine: he would understand the Trinity or the Incarnation or predestination; he would impose his hypothetical understanding of the Epistle to the Romans or the composition of the Bible. Both heretic and schismatic are outside the church: they decline from a higher level than the rest of the world, and so their decline is at first imperceptible; but the floodgates have been opened; the faith and the custodian of the faith have been attacked; and it is only for the ordinary processes of decline to bring about the *corruptio optimi pessima*. Because the new pagan has lived on levels unknown to the old, because his mind has ventured into broader realms and his heart known deeper aspirations, so his attempts to attain satisfaction are more thorough and more hopeless than the ancient world could ever know.

Four aspects of the progress of the church call for attention.[40]

40 In what we have here, only three aspects are mentioned. The document is clearly incomplete, as is obvious from the opening list of eight sections. As noted above in note 1, not only is this section incomplete; the final section, 'The multiple dialectic,' does not appear at all.

There is the enucleation of the *depositum fidei* that is called the development of dogma. It is the accumulation of the anathemas against heretics, the discovery of distinctions implicit in vital practice yet not formulated by the mind, the formation of definitions as distinct elements are recognized, compared, classified, correlated, and the ordering of the whole into a body of Christian doctrine. This progress resembles the progress of the reason, inasmuch as it is not revolutionary like that of the understanding but a gradual advance towards refinement. But it is not to be concluded from this resemblance that the development of dogma is simply a matter of deduction in the mind: it is a vital movement of the church itself, casting off what is incompatible with itself under the guidance of the Spirit, learning from conflict differences that always existed but before had passed unnoticed, and reflecting upon its own life history to become ever more fully conscious of what in reality the church is.

Next we may consider the development of Christian spirituality. Here is even more apparent a vital growth. The substance of a passionate desire for assimilation to Christ shines equally in martyrs and virgins, monks and preachers, in every age. But the accidents change with the age, with the changing particulars of times and situations, in the fashion of intuitive adaptation. While all is bound together by the solidity of a tradition that would send the student of sources of the latest book through the treatises and hagiographies of twenty centuries.

Intimately connected with the above, yet distinct, is the development of works of charity and the apostolate. They date from the beginning, but we wish to draw attention to them here because in Catholic Action and missiology we think may be recognized an enlargement of conception and a reform of method that would indicate that the church has moved into the sphere of 'reflex history.'

7 Analytic Concept of History, in Blurred Outline[1]

1 What is meant by an analytic concept of history?
   (a) Concepts of apprehension and concepts of understanding
   (b) Analytic and synthetic acts of understanding
   (c) Logical and real, static and dynamic, analysis
   (d) Progress of understanding
   (e) What is meant by an analytic concept of history?
2 What is the essence of history?
   (a) History and historiography
   (b) Material and formal objects of history
   (c) The formal object of an analytic concept of history
3 The unity of history: the dialectic
   (a) The nature of the dialectic
   (b) The form of the dialectic
   (c) Rates of the dialectic
   (d) Existence of the dialectic
   (e) Division of the dialectic
4 Analysis of the dialectic
   (a) Formal analysis of the dialectic
   (b) Dynamic analysis of the dialectic

---

1 See above, p. 95, note 1. Lonergan's original manuscript is available in digital form on www.bernardlonergan.com at 71307DTE030. And see below, p. 154, note 1. See also Shute, *Origins* 121–44.

1 What is meant by an analytic concept of history?

(a) Concepts of apprehension and concepts of understanding [2]

By the concept of apprehension, we know what the object is, and we know what it is not. We do not know why it is what it is.

Example: most definitions are of this type, especially in the inductive sciences. From such definitions nothing can be deduced, except by 'descending induction,' which wavers between *petitio principii* and a guess.[3]

By the concept of the understanding, we know what makes the object what it is.

2 See below, p. 156, note 5.
3 See below, p. 156, note 6.

Such knowledge is a premise to further knowledge. The definition of the circle is knowledge of what makes the circle a circle: from it the properties of the circle may be deduced.

(b) Analytic and synthetic acts of understanding

Any human act of understanding is the apperceptive unity of a many.

If the many in question is concrete and particular, we have a synthetic act of understanding.

Example: Christopher Dawson's historical essays, Newman's illative sense.[4]

If the many is abstract and universal, we have the analytic act of understanding. Examples in what follows.

(c) Logical and real, static and dynamic, analysis

The 'many' known in the unity of an analytic concept may be a logical or a real multiplicity; and in the latter case, the realities may be static or dynamic. Examples:

The essential definition of man, 'rational animal,' is a logical multiplicity: genus and difference.

The chemist's definitions of material substances are based on the real multiplicity of their material causes.

The Thomist metaphysician understands limited being as a compound of existence and essence: his multiplicity is real but static.

The Newtonian astronomer's understanding of planetary motion as a resultant of different accelerations on a moving mass is an analytic concept based upon a real and dynamic multiplicity.

(d) Progress of understanding

Intellectus procedit a maius generali ad maius particulare, per actus incompletos ad actum perfectum.[5]

---

4 On Newman's illative sense, see Newman, *An Essay in Aid of a Grammar of Assent*, chapter 9. For Dawson, see, for example, Christopher Dawson, *Enquiries into Religion and Culture* (London and New York: Sheed & Ward, 1933).
5 See Thomas Aquinas, *Summa theologiae*, 1, q. 85, a. 3.

First we understand things diagrammatically, in outline, from the fundamental point of view: then we fill in the details.

This is true of all understanding: but it is to be complemented by the fact that the understanding proceeds from thesis through antithesis to higher synthesis until it attains its proper most general form. Of this more later.[6]

(e) What is meant by an analytic concept of history?

In terms of the distinctions drawn above, an Analytic Concept of History may be described as

(a') an act of understanding, not merely knowing what history is, but knowing what makes it what it is;

(b') an analytic act of understanding: proceeding not from historical fact to synthesis, but from an analysis of human nature;

(c') where this analysis gives a real, not a logical, and a dynamic, not a static, multiplicity: thus it should result, not in the categories of the metaphysicians but in something like the causally and chronologically interrelated view of the astronomer; this, because it analyzes not being but action;

(d') finally, in an Analytic Concept of History we aim only at the first and most general act of understanding with regard to history.

2 *What is the essence of history?*

(a) [History and historiography] distinguish: history that is written (history books) and history that is written about (persons, peoples, events)

We are concerned only with the latter.

(b) Material and formal objects of history

The material object of history is the aggregate of human actions: all that all men think or say or do.

---

6 Handwritten at this point: 'Cf. 5 (c).' See below, pp. 137–38.

The formal object of history is the material object submitted to a selective process. This process is defined by the principle: An event is *historic*[7] in the measure in which it influences human action.

Hence, remembering the reciprocity of cause and effect, we may say that history essentially is the course of human action in its causes.

To the historian, this definition may well seem strange: it does so because it defines, not what the historian attains, but the ideal towards which he tends. Only in terms of this ideal can the selection of fact in any written history be accounted for.

(c) The formal object of an analytic concept of history

To raise history to the level of a pure science, it is necessary to refine upon the formal object defined above; this, as follows:

First, because there is no science of the particular, we must prescind from persons and peoples to concentrate upon events. We cannot answer the question, Who does it? We attempt to answer, within the generality of our inquiry, What is done?

Second, because the action of the First Cause, though more excellent in itself, is less known to us, we confine ourselves to the secondary causes of history.

This, however, without prejudice to a hypothetical consideration of the supernatural virtues and the conditions of their emergence.

Third, among secondary causes, we distinguish essential and accidental, to omit the latter.

Among accidental causes are disturbances of the normal order: plagues, famines, earthquakes, floods. We do not deny that such an event as the Black Death had vast repercussions: our position is simply that such accidents do not concern pure science of history. Similarly, with regard to racist theories, which if true are very important historically: it remains that their influence is not in the essence of history but that of an accident interfering with essential history; further, as regards scientific inquiry they pertain to biology.

The essential secondary causes of history are human wills: not indeed in their immanent merits and demerits, but in their effective transience, by which man makes and unmakes man both directly and indirectly.

---

7 In the typescript this word is all in upper-case letters.

Fourth, in the essential secondary causes, human wills, we distinguish between formal and material import.

Roughly, this is a distinction between vectors that give the magnitude and direction of forces and, on the other hand, friction.

Formally, the will concerns history insofar as it is exerted upon the manner of life.

Materially, the will concerns history insofar as it is exerted upon the fact of life: this is the will to live, let live, propagate. Without it there is no history.

To resume, the formal object of an analytic concept of history is the course of history as determined by the human will in its decisions upon manner of living.

3 The unity of history: The dialectic

In the previous section we have attained a logical unity as the object of our investigation. But real analysis presupposes a real unity: we cannot study the human will in the abstract, nor human wills in the aggregate, but must find some underlying principle of unity before we can begin to analyze. Hence we speak of the dialectic.

(a) The nature of the dialectic

By the dialectic we do not mean Plato's orderly conversation, nor Hegel's expansion of concepts, nor Marx's fiction of an alternative to mechanical materialism.

We do mean something like a series of experiments, a process of trial and error. Not indeed the formal experiment of the laboratory, for man is not so master of his fate. Rather, an inverted experiment, in which *objective reality molds the mind of man into conformity with itself*.[8]

Here, 'objective reality' does not mean 'material reality' but all reality, and especially Reality.

Further, the 'molding' is no obscure influence, but the simple imposition of the rewards of knowledge, truth, righteousness, and the penalties of ignorance, error, sin.

8 In the typescript these italicized words are all in upper-case letters.

(b) The form of the dialectic

We have defined the dialectic by the interaction of the mind and reality.

Hence the form of the dialectic is the succession of objective situation, thought, action, new situation, new thought, etc., etc.

Plainly, if the thought is poor, the situation will go from bad to worse: and this most easily happens when the evil lies in the spiritual order and so does not immediately manifest its effects.

On the other hand, if the thought is good, the situation advances from good to better: and this most easily happens when the good is of the material order, manifest and palpable.

(c) Rates of the dialectic

The dialectic presupposes that the thought governing action and bringing forth situations will react to its product, to eliminate the evil and improve the good.

In the very long run this would seem true, but its truth is not necessary. On the contrary, decline, as we shall see, tends per se to a degradation and stagnation that bring essential history to a standstill.

On the other hand, as will come for observation later, the earlier stages of major decline, which attacks fundamental principles and cuts society adrift, are marked by a feverish activity of the dialectic.

(d) Existence of the dialectic

The existence of the dialectic is a matter of 'more and less,' of form in matter.

The principles of its existence seem as follows.

First, the will follows the intellect.

There are indeed rebellions, but these are not the rule but the exception: and what is exceptional is to pure theory accidental. It is true that the exceptions may become the rule, but then there is a prior perversion of the intellect by the will, so that we come back to our principle that the will follows the intellect.

Second, the intellect tends to uniformity.

It tends to uniformity radically because the intellect is a potency and its actuation is not the achievement of individuals but of the race. What the angelic intellect attains in the instant of *aevum*, man attains in the whole of time. Thus essentially human knowledge is the maintenance of a tradition, and inquiry that increases knowledge, as genius that integrates it, are not fine flowerings of individualism but, on the larger view, products of the age and instruments of the race in its development.

The mechanism of this radical tendency to uniformity of intellects is human dependence upon its environment, geographical and social. We make ourselves, not out of ourselves, but out of our environments. We make ourselves, for the will is free; but not out of ourselves, for what is moved is moved extrinsically. Hence the impressive difference between being brought up in Mayfair and in the jungle: all of us are dependent upon others for most of our knowledge; most of our reactions and responses are imitations; most of our judgments are repetitions.

In this influence of the environment it is well to distinguish between the direct and the indirect action of man on man.

By direct action we mean convincing of the true, persuading to what is right, indoctrinating with falsehood, conspiring to evil, and finally, to give words the glow of efficacy, a judicious use of force.

By indirect action we refer to the fact that the social situation created by the past specifies and imposes the problems to be faced by the present.

The former is the action of education, laws, theatre, cinema, press, wireless, and concentration camps.

The latter is the action of the wisdom and folly of our ancestors, and other people's, concretely in our midst in the form of institutions, customs, habits, mentalities, characters.

(e) Division of the dialectic

We shall speak of the single and the multiple dialectic.

The single dialectic is the dialectic within the cultural channel of mutual influence constituted by the social unit.

The multiple dialectic is the dialectic of the single dialectics, in their transferences, their interactions, their synthetic unity in the whole course of history.

We may note that the single dialectic, because confined to the social unit, is marked by a reinforcement of the tendency to uniformity of intellects. For within the social unit, men not only tend to think alike: they are also forced in a thousand ways to act as though they did, so that the historical significance of the dissenter from the 'generally accepted' does not lie in the present, where his influence is small, but potentially in the future, when his views may be part of generally accepted views.

4 Analysis of the dialectic

(a) Formal analysis of the dialectic

The dialectic is the aggregate of human actions in their interdependence in the present and in their solidarity with the past and the future.

Accordingly, a formal analysis of the dialectic coincides with a division of human actions.

The most general division of human actions is: actions according to nature; actions contrary to nature; actions above nature.

This division is metaphysically ultimate: its categories are the intelligible to man, the unintelligible *simpliciter*, the too intelligible for man. Such a division is ultimate, for it is based on the confines of our intelligence, and so excludes the possibility of higher synthesis.

N.B. In stating that action contrary to nature is unintelligible, we do not mean that it is unknowable. Sin is the possible object of apprehension and judgment; it is not a possible object of understanding. For the understanding is the faculty by which we know the 'why a thing is what it is.' But sin admits no explanation: it is the desertion of reason and has no reason that is more than a pretense.

Why did the angels sin? Why did Adam sin? There is no 'why.' We do not say there is a 'why' but we cannot know it: we say there is no 'why' to be known. We do not say God had not excellent reasons for permitting it, so we do not evacuate the *mysterium iniquitatis*; on the contrary, we add another, which, however, is a mystery not from excess of intelligibility but from lack of it.

Cf. 'Nemo ex me scire quaerat, quod me nescire scio; nisi forte ut nescire discat, quod sciri non posse sciendum est.'[9]

N.B. (2) The distinction between the unintelligibility of sin and the too-intelligibility of grace is the Light-darkness contrast of the New Testament.

(b) Dynamic analysis of the dialectic

The transition from the above formal analysis to dynamic analysis coincides with the transition from a consideration of human actions to a consideration of them as they are in the dialectic. This we attempt as follows:

9 See above, p. 105, note 15.

First, we ask, What would be the course of history were all human actions according to nature yet without the support of grace?

We consider a purely ideal case, to draw a purely ideal line for the course of history: this procedure may be illustrated by Newton's First Law, that a body continues to move in a straight line with uniform speed as long as no extrinsic force intervenes.[10]

Second, we ask, What is the deviation from the ideal line of history that follows from actions contrary to nature?

Third, we ask, What would be the principle of renaissance that would offset decline and restore the progress of nature?

Fourth, we consider the combinations of these in the single and the multiple dialectics.

5 *The ideal line of history*

(a) Definition of the ideal line

The ideal line is history on the supposition that all men in all thoughts, words, deeds, observe the natural law, and do so without the aid of grace.

It envisages, then, a state of pure nature, in which men as a matter of fact do not sin, though on the one hand they are not destined to a supernatural end and, on the other, do not stand in need of the *gratia sanans* that counteracts the wounds of original sin.

(b) General character of the ideal line

We are concerned with the history of man, not insofar as he is an animal, for that pertains to biology, but insofar as he differs from the animal.

Our object is, then, man's performance of his earthly task insofar as this is the work of intellect and will.

But methodologically we have eliminated from the scope of this section any consideration of the will: *ex hypothesi* it always operates ideally.

Further, we consider this action of man from the viewpoint of history: that is, we consider it not insofar as it is a routine but insofar as it is diversified.

10 See above, p. 103 and note 13.

Now the diversification of human action, as it proceeds from the intellect, is manifestly a consequence of the progress of the intellect. Accordingly, the general character of the ideal line of history is its determination by the progress of the human intellect.

We have, then, to determine first the line of development of the mind of man, and from this the ideal line of history.

(c) The line of the development of the human mind

The mind of man is a conscious potency conditioned by sense.

Because it is a potency, there is progress diversifying the routine of life.

Because it is a conscious potency, there are two types of its activity: spontaneous and reflex.

Further, because the reflex use of intellect presupposes the erection of canons of thought and of methods of investigation, it follows that first there is a period of spontaneous thought and second a period of reflex thought.

Because the intellect is a potency conditioned by sense, we may roughly distinguish two fields of knowledge.

There is the philosophic field, in which thought depends upon the mere fact of experience (metaphysic) or upon its broad and manifest characters (cosmology, rational psychology, ethics).

Second, there is the scientific field, in which thought depends not upon the generalities of experience but upon its details, and these examined with the greatest care and accuracy.

Finally, roughly corresponding to these two fields of thought are two methods or manners of thought: deduction and induction.

Now deductive thought proceeds in a straight line; inductive proceeds in a series of revolutions from theses through antitheses to higher syntheses till finally the highest synthesis is reached and thought becomes deductive.

Deductive proceeds in a straight line: its progress is essentially a matter of greater refinement and accuracy. But there is an exception: even in the deductive field there is an initial wavering till the proper most general terms are found. There were philosophers before Aristotle. More interesting is the fact that mathematics, though a deductive science, has been undergoing revolutions: but this would seem simply to be due to the generalization of the concepts of number and space.

Inductive thought proceeds by thesis, antithesis, higher synthesis.

This follows from the nature of the understanding, the intellectual light that reveals the one in the many.

For *intellectus est per se infallibilis*; but de facto understanding is of reality, not as it is in itself, but as it is apprehended by us.[11]

The initial understanding that constitutes the thesis is true of the facts insofar as they are known: but knowledge of them is not adequate. Further apprehension will give rise to antithesis. Further understanding to higher synthesis.

We may note that there are two ways of being certain through understanding.

First, we may be certain if we understand in a highest possible synthesis. For to the highest possible, there can be no antithesis.

Again, we may be certain if we understand what we know in one of Newman's real apprehensions: for a real apprehension involves a grasp of all possibly pertinent fact and so excludes the possibility of antithesis.

(d) Deduction of the ideal line of history

The basis of our deduction is the distinction, chronological as well as real, of spontaneous and reflex thought, and the laws of deductive and inductive thought.

From the distinction of spontaneous thought and reflex may be deduced the three periods of ideal history:

(1) Spontaneous history
(2) The development of reflex thought
(3) Reflex history

Spontaneous history is marked in the deductive field by popular religion and morality, and in the inductive by the development of agriculture and the mechanical arts, the evolution of economic and political structures from barter to exchange and the tribe to the state, and the cult of the fine arts and humanism. Of the elements of the progress in the inductive field, the first two are solidary, while the last is the fruit of the leisure they make possible.

The higher culture gives birth to philosophy and science, and so to the expansion of reflex thought. In the deductive field religion and morality are placed on a philosophic basis. In the inductive there is the

11 See above, pp. 108–109 and note 24.

development of science and its application to all the practical problems of existence. This gives rise to a more abundant and universally distributed leisure and so opens the way to a still higher culture.

Reflex history begins not with reflex thought about history but with the social consciousness that the earthly task of man is the making of man, giving him his body, the conditions of his activity, the material from which he must draw in the fashioning of his soul. Thus reflex history is the deliberate and social direction of human activity to its immediate goal: history, the making of man by man.

We would insist upon the essentially social character of this reflex history. It is not enough for a Plato to inquire into the Ideal Republic. What is wanted is a social enthusiasm for the ideal society, such as marked the eighteenth-century Enlightenment, the liberal dogma of 'progress,' the communist insistence on 'class consciousness,' and the Catholic doctrines of the mystical body of Christ and the social kingship of Christ, as applied to Catholic Action (transformation of the social 'milieu' at home) and missionary activity (such a transformation abroad).

We cannot be expected to characterize 'reflex history' as we have the preceding, simply by stating what is done. But the following points seem capable of deduction.

Reflex history (of the ideal line of history) would be marked in the deductive field by a philosophic determination of its 'general line.' Its 'general line' would not coincide with that determined by Stalin,[12] but its principle, its idea, would be similar. And plainly this 'general line' would simply be a philosophy of history.

In the inductive field, which is the field of practical activity, reflex history would be marked by ordered freedom.

First, the order that holds distinct the deductive and inductive fields of thought till finally the stage is reached when all knowledge reaches its unity.

Second, the order that corresponds to the development attained by man. For the greater the progress, the greater the differentiation of occupation, the more complex the social structure organizing these differences to the general end, [and][13] the wider the extent of the unit.

12 See Shute, *Origins* 131–32 and note 495: 'Stalin's "general line" is informed by the scientific laws, determined through Marxist materialist analysis. See Robert C. Tucker, "Stalinism and Transformation," in *Stalin*, ed. T.H. Rigby (Englewood Cliffs, NJ: Prentice-Hall, Inc., 1966), pp. 58–67.'
13 See below, p. 167.

Third, the order that keeps the virtue of progress in the virtuous mean. The power of intellect is the domination of the universal over the material many: its exploitation is hierarchy. But man is not intellect, and he must not permit himself to be led by the nose in his progress; else the term of his efforts would be exceedingly intelligible but utterly inhuman.

Besides order, freedom also.

First, the freedom that comes of *autoliberazione*, the self-renouncing will that makes its goal the infinitely nuanced 'better' of progress. The forces of law and order can only take care of the exceptions: a nation cannot be indicted.

Second, the freedom that leaves the maximum of initiative to the individual. Only the conspiracy of all human intelligences can discover the 'better' of progress, which is concrete and particular. Only the individual can bear the risks that all essays at progress involve: the totalitarian state cannot run the risks of progress; it can imitate, it can perfect, but its initiations are too vast to be anything but clumsy, and its execution of plans too blind to be anything but brutal.

N.B. (1) The last contention may seem untrue. The totalitarian states may be thought to be doing rather nicely. But this view can be based only upon the material improvements they effect: that is simply imitating and perfecting. The real problem of today is not material improvement but social relationship: the development of socially minded man. The performances of the totalitarian states, especially Russia and Germany, in this field are puerile, a mass of apparently useful lies.

N.B. (2) We have overlooked the difference between the theses, antitheses, and syntheses of thought, on the one hand, and of action on the other.

The theses of thought may be simply false. The theses of action cannot be simply false: else they could never be brought into action. But they are incomplete: glimpses of the true that bring partial good. As a simple example, we may take classical education as a thesis which finds its antithesis in the modern side.

6 Decline

(a) Nature and goal of decline

Decline is systematic deviation from the ideal line of history.

The ideal line is determined by universal observance of the natural law.

Not every violation of the natural law is an element of decline, but only such violation as is systematic.

What then is meant by 'systematic' violation of the natural law? We recall the point made above (cf. 3, d [p. 133]) that the will follows the intellect: more precisely, that formal rebellions of the will against the intellect are of their nature casual and accidental and so do not concern pure theory. In other words, when men sin against their consciences, their sins are exceptions to a rule they recognize and a law they habitually tend to observe. But when they deform their consciences, then their sins are not exceptions to a rule but instances of what has become the rule.

Decline, then, as a systematic deviation, is the deformation of the social conscience, the interchange of right and wrong in the 'generally accepted' views of the dialectic. Cf. Isaias 5.20–23.[14]

We note that it is outside the limits of our inquiry to determine the degree of culpability in the individual's acceptance of the common view: with regard to this point the distinction between primary and secondary elements in the moral law is important.

All that concerns us is that this deformation of the social conscience exists, and that the number of individuals who successfully resist accepting it hardly is sufficient to justify consideration in general theory.

Nemo repente summus. Like everything else in the world, the deformation of the social conscience takes place gradually. Nonetheless, it tends to a definite goal: the animalization of man.

By sin man repudiates reason. Decline realizes this repudiation. The cumulative effects of systematic sin empty out of the world's philosophy every principle that raises man above the beast. And with the principles gone, the will to be more than a beast is stultified. For the only ideal that can be set before such a will is the ideal of the beast.

Progress, the principle of diversification in history, diversifies this animalization of man. The decadent savage and Nebuchodonosor [*sic*], Nero and the New Paganism threatening Germany, differ vastly. But they are radically the same: the animalization of man on different levels of history.

A surmise: the 'beast' of the apocalypse is the animalization of man in reflex history. In what stage?

14 NRSV: 'Ah, you who call evil good and good evil, who put darkness for light and light for darkness, who put bitter for sweet and sweet for bitter! Ah, you who are wise in your own eyes, and shrewd in your own sight! Ah, you who are heroes in drinking wine and valiant at mixing drink, who acquit the guilty for a bribe, and deprive the innocent of their rights!'

(b) Division of decline

Decline divides into minor and major.

Minor decline is the deformation of conscience on the practical level of inductive thought.

Major decline is the deformation of conscience on the theoretical level of deductive thought.[15]

The combination and interaction of major and minor will be referred to as compound decline.

(c) Minor decline

Radix omnium malorum cupiditas. We are concerned not with cupidity in itself but with the distortion it engenders in the intellect. Egoism is hardly separate from egocentricity. Thus, enlightened self-interest seems practically a contradiction in terms, for self-interest puts self at the center of the universe, and that is not the center. Self-interest cannot be enlightened because it is not objective.[16]

This bias of practical thought together with the differences of ability, opportunity, and power that are inherent in nature and any form of society results in the reality the communists name the 'class war.'

The mechanism that transforms the distinction between those favored by fortune more and those favored less into a social abyss would seem as follows.

First, the new syntheses of progress have three disadvantages:

(1) it is not clear they offer the better, for concrete issues are complex;
(2) it is manifest they threaten the liquidation of what are vested interests;
(3) in most cases they contain an element of risk and demand the spirit that contemns the sheltered life, insured from tip to toe.

Second, by reason of their advantages, the favored are able to solve the antitheses that stand against their own progressive well-being. By reason of their egocentricity, they barely think of solving any others. The

15 See above, p. 111, note 25.
16 See above, p. 111, note 27.

bourgeois is full of the milk of human kindness: but this bias in outlook makes him pronounce nonexistent or insoluble the antitheses that do not directly affect him.

Third, the depressed are not merely left behind but they are degraded by a set of palliatives invented to ease the bourgeois conscience and to provide for the security of the nation a more or less sturdy and contented populace.

The result is disorder. Both the progress of the few and the backwardness of the many are distorted. The progress is distorted by its narrow basis and unnatural exclusiveness. The backwardness is distorted by the successive layers of senseless palliatives.

And this disorder is not merely some abstract grievance waiting on mere good will and kind words to be set right. It is the concrete and practically ineradicable form of the social structure, of achievements, institutions, customs, habits, mentalities, characters.

(d) Major decline

Minor decline has its root in our not loving our neighbors as ourselves, in our not taking the viewpoint of pure intellect and seeing all men (self included) as instances of a universal.

Major decline proceeds through the deformation of conscience to the dethronement of the reason.

The causes of the deformation of conscience are both subjective and objective.

The subjective cause is self-justification. Man within himself naturally desires the peace and harmony of unity. But his actions are often sinful. He is thus in the dilemma of conforming his actions to his conscience by doing penance, or, on the other hand, conforming his conscience to his actions by the radical self-justification that denies sin to be sin.

The objective cause of deformation of conscience is the unintelligibility of sin. Men sin, and their sins are objective elements in the social situation. What ought not to be, is. This objective unintelligibility confronts the just with an insoluble problem: if he recognizes the *fait accompli*, he cooperates with injustice; if he refuses to recognize it, then he creates for himself an imaginary world in which he cannot live. But to the unjust, such situations are but proof, palpable and manifest, of his denial of sin to be sin. The moral law is all very well in theory, but obviously out of the question in practice.

This divorce of theory and practice in favor of bad practice is naturally followed by a conformation of theory to bad practice.

Here the causes are the same as above, at least radically.

There is the subjective cause. But this, instead of the desire for unity of consciousness, is the desire for unity of thought and action.

There is the objective cause. For the theorist of bad practice is a realist. He considers man not as he ought to be, but man as he actually is. And this real man supplies abundant evidence to confirm the ever-bolder views that are put forward at each stage in the relaxation of the moral code.

Thus, for example, the liberal economists worked out their theory on the assumption that the only motive that could be effective for the majority of men is self-interest. It is an assumption that probably is 99 percent true, but the omission of the 1 percent results in a radical vitiation of method. For in thinking of men you must think of them as they ought to be; if you think of them as they are, you will make them far worse than they need be.

Implicit in the deformation of conscience is the dethronement of reason.

This, however, is not manifested by a rejection of reason but by the invasion of the understanding, with its seductive syntheses and *Weltanschauungen*, into the deductive field of thought.

Here, however, we have not a process of thesis, antithesis, and higher synthesis, but simply *a succession of lower syntheses*.

The mechanism of this is as follows.

Society is in decline, but at no instant desires more than it already has of decadence. The traditional virtues are praised as long as they can be kept. Thus, the theorist, to sell his wares, bundles them along with what people are known to want. And because people want less and less, the successive bundles or syntheses or views contain less and less.

In the succession of lower syntheses, we must distinguish between the nominal survivals and the new arrivals.[17] Since the breakup of Christendom we have had Protestantism, Deism, Liberalism, Naturalism, Communism, Racism. These have been new arrivals in their day. Since, they have each been watered down and accommodated to most new winds of doctrine.

17 The expression may be based on the title of one of Hilaire Belloc's books, *Survivals and New Arrivals* (New York: The Macmillan Company, 1929).

Each of the successive lower syntheses is accompanied by a 'mysticism.' For none is equal to reality. None is recommended by more than its resemblance to the old and its apparent conformity to the new. To make up the deficit there is the halo of fiction and legend, the appeal to enthusiasm, slander for the opposition, and, if need be, persecution, which later is piously and completely forgotten.

As Mr Christopher Hollis elegantly puts it: When in traveling across the world you meet a new lie, you know you are in contact with another culture.[18]

(e) Compound decline

Both minor accelerates major and major minor.

Minor accelerates major, inasmuch as it supplies the mechanism for the imposition of the successive lower syntheses.

The tension between liberal and conservative, the struggle between privileged and depressed, takes on a cosmic significance, when the disputes of major decline sponsor slogans for rival cupidities and hatreds. The French Revolution made the lay state a reality. The Russian puts militant atheism in terms of bread and butter.

Major accelerates minor.

It deprives practical thought and science of the guidance of philosophy. Of itself, minor decline tends to disorder; coupled with major its goal is an unintelligible chaos. Sin is unintelligible: its fruit is no mere antithesis to be swallowed by some higher synthesis, but an indigestible morsel, refractory to intellect, and admitting no remedy except liquidation.

N.B. We omitted to note, with reference to the successive lower syntheses, that the new arrivals are often based upon, or at least exploit, the new achievements of progress.

---

18 See Christopher Hollis, *We Aren't So Dumb* (London and New York: Longmans, Green & Co., 1937) 179, where one character in a dialogue says, 'What is a nation? Race, religion, language – none of these cover it. It is a group of people that tell the same sort of lie, and when on your travels you come to a new lie, you know that you have come to a new culture.' See Bernard Lonergan, *Shorter Writings*, vol. 20 in Collected Works of Bernard Lonergan, ed. Robert C. Croken, Robert M. Doran, and H. Daniel Monsour (Toronto: University of Toronto Press, 2007) 113, note 3, where the editors had not yet identified the reference.

It must be remembered that decline is not something in itself, a deviation from the ideal line that is a new and distinct line; on the contrary it is simply the distortion and the ultimate stultification of progress.

7 Renaissance

(a) Accidental and essential renaissance

It is commonly thought by people watching the houses of others burn that their own could not. The excesses of the French Revolution or the Spanish Civil War are attributed to the mysterious Latin temperament. The excesses of the Russian revolution are too incredible to be believed, and so they have a poor press. But nothing like that could happen in our own country: our people have too much common sense.

With regard to this point of view we observe:

Temperament no doubt makes a difference in the accidental details of a historical movement. But no people is saved by temperament from the implications of its subjective beliefs and its objective social situation. Whether these implications work out with a bloodstained fanfare or by the elegant shift by which the left wing of one generation becomes the right wing of the next is of no concern to pure theory.

We do not believe, then, in the possibility of 'muddling through' the crises of history.

By accidental renaissance we understand the rebirth of progress after decline in virtue of the effacing effects of time.

As long as the disorder and the falsehoods of decline persist, there is no reason to believe in the possibility of a rebirth of progress. This rebirth is conditioned by a dark age, in which the old error is forgotten and the old evil obliterated. Then man, by severing himself from his past, can begin again.

Manifestly, this is a chance renewal, an accidental rebirth.

By essential renaissance we understand the emergence in human society of a principle that will enable man directly to face and counteract decline and deliberately to restore progress.

(b) The nature of essential renaissance

Progress is the thesis of nature, the product of the natural law.

Decline is the antithesis of sin.

To find the higher synthesis of these two, we must go beyond the confines of the natural order. It is not the mind of man that can make issue with the unintelligibility of sin and the dethronement of the mind itself.

Hence, it is the nature of essential renaissance to transcend the natural order, to be a 'new order.'

(Cf. Trotskyist continual revolution.)[19]

(c) The characteristics of essential renaissance

What transcends man is to man as man is to the beast, the beast is to the plant, the plant to the element. Cf. Thornton, *The Incarnate Lord*.[20]

From this follow the four characteristics of essential renaissance, the principles of a new 'higher criticism' to replace the Hegelian.

First, the new order would be knowable: man knows being, and outside that category there is nothing.

Second, the new order would be mystery: it would be to the understanding of man as that understanding is to the brute, *ta epekeina*.

Third, man could not raise himself into the new order: nothing can transcend itself.

Fourth, on analogy, in the new order man's nature would not be negated but included in a higher synthesis. Just as man, as a mass of matter, is subject to the laws of mechanics; as alive, is subject to the laws of organisms; as sentient, has the perceptions and the appetites of the brute: so in the new order, the laws of specifically human nature remain, though transcended and included in what is higher.

Thus, man's acceptance of the new order must be rational, and so evidence of its emergence must be provided (miracles). Man's attainment of his end remains dependent upon his immanent merits and demerits, though the conditions of his activity remain social. Etc.

(d) Further characteristics of essential renaissance

In the preceding paragraph we considered renaissance in itself, that is, as transcending: we have now to determine its characteristics in its relation to progress and decline, that is, as renaissance.

19 See above, p. 117, note 34.
20 Lionel Spencer Thornton, *The Incarnate Lord: An Essay Concerning the Doctrine of the Incarnation in Its Relation to Organic Conception* (London: Longmans, Green & Co., 1928). Lonergan's reference to this work was written by hand.

Now, as the restoration of progress coincides, really, with counteracting decline, these characteristics of the 'new order' may be deduced from their opposition to the causes of decline.

Thus, against self-justification the new order will set penance: the new order will be a rebirth of man in which the old man is renounced.

Second, against the objective unintelligibility of the social situation, the new order will set faith in the too-intelligibility of its transcendence.

Third, against the successive ambiguities of the dialectic, which brings forth both the higher syntheses of progress and the lower syntheses of decline, the new order will set a living authority providentially infallible.

Fourth, against the dethronement of reason the new order will present its own rigorous and all-embracing rationalism under the higher synthesis of faith and authority.

Fifth, against economic determinism and the despair it engenders, the new order will bring hope for its transcending good, lifting man above the *engrenage* of cupidity by a higher goal.

Sixth, against the egoism of minor decline, the new order will set justice-transcending charity.

Seventh, to make this charity real and effective, the new order will preach its counsels, whose spirit is for all, whose actuality is for a group impressive both in number and quality.

Poverty against cupidity.

Chastity against the beast.

Obedience against the revolutionary spirit of self-will.

(e) The 'new order' and men

The Greeks said that power revealed the man. The 'new order' is a deeper assaying. 'And this is the judgment: Because the light is come into the world and men loved darkness rather than the light. For their works were evil. For everyone that doth evil hateth the light and cometh not to the light, that his works may not be reproved. But he that doth truth cometh to the light, that his works may be made manifest: because they are done in God' (John 3.19–21).

Truly, in the dialectic of major decline, men are as sheep without a shepherd. The eternal verities and the primary precepts of morality withstand the lies of decadent culture. If their hearts are true, the voice of the Good Shepherd is known and welcome to them, for the song of the new order is: Glory to God in the highest, and on earth peace to men of good will.

8 The multiple dialectic

(a) Single and multiple dialectics

The single dialectic is the succession, within the social unit, of situation, thought, action, new situation, new thought, etc.

The multiple dialectic is the aggregate of single dialectics in their synthetic unity.

(b) Single dialectic without grace

Progress is of nature; decline is the cumulative effect of sin.

Hence the course of the single dialectic without grace is an initial progress that gradually is distorted and then submerged in the flood of decline.

This curve – first ascending, then descending – is accentuated by the law of the priority of the economic as a condition: for a higher culture presupposes a higher economic development to liberate man more fully from material cares. The accentuation of the curve arises from the fact that to labor and sacrifice for economic improvement is easy, to do so for the impalpable benefits of culture is difficult. Thus man achieves the first and barely attempts the second.[21]

Hence the single dialectic without grace is: first, economic development and social organization; second, cultural advance and social disintegration; third, the animalization of man on the higher level of his achievement.

We may note that this corresponds to Spengler's analogy of organic growth and decay.[22]

(c) Multiple dialectic without grace

The transition from the single dialectics to the multiple may be made by a consideration of transference and reaction.

Transference is the importation into a social unit of the attainments and/or miseries of another.

21 This sentence is added by hand.
22 The reference is to the relation between culture and 'civilization' in Oswald Spengler, *The Decline of the West*, trans. Charles Francis Atkinson (London: Allen & Unwin, 1926; New York: Knopf, 1957).

Transference is real or formal: real in the cases of migration and conquest; formal in the case of imitation – importation of ideas.

Formal transference is spatial or temporal: spatial between contemporaries; temporal, when it is the inheritance from a culture now in decay or extinct.

Reaction commonly denotes opposition to progress or decline within the social unit. Here we use it to denote opposition to the importation of progress (unhealthy reaction) or of decline (healthy reaction).

Next we may note the following general laws of transference.

(1) Improvements in the material order are easily transferred; the limitation is the capacity of the importer to acquire the requisite skill or science.

(2) The disorder of minor decline is essentially a domestic product and hardly admits of transference.

(3) An intense national spirit resists everything that is not demonstrably superior to its own achievement. The Japanese admit the monkey theory for the origin of foreigners; they themselves are descended from God. The ancient Romans chased the deputation from the Academy out of the city.

However, such a spirit is not immune from its own decline: and so two centuries later Rome was becoming the home of all the crazy cults from the East.

(4) As to the transference of reflex thought, we observe:

First, sound philosophic or scientific thought is incompatible with major decline, for major decline is false philosophy, and the basis of science is philosophy;

Second, because major decline thus enters into the very texture of reflex thought, it is impossible to transfer the thought without transferring the decline.

Now from these general laws of transference we may deduce the general laws of the multiple dialectic without grace.

First, transference with healthy reaction, a matter of national spirit, results in *the continuity of human progress* despite the fact that each progressive people in turn succumbs to decline.

Second, transference without healthy reaction *universalizes decline*: it makes the backward people *brûler l'étape* in the downward course of decline. Thus Russia under the Soviets expiates the sins of the West.

Third, migration of a people is equivalent to transference with healthy reaction: it plants the old culture in a fresh world. On the other hand, conquest tends to be simply a universalization of decline.

Fourth, resistance to major decline despite conquest requires the influence of the 'new order.' Cf. the Jews in captivity or under Antiochus, the Poles and the Irish in modern history. We may note that in the spontaneous period of ancient history, major decline is the multiplication and then the degradation of the gods. Cf. CTS pamphlets, A Philosophy of the History of Religions.[23]

Fifth, a people that lives under pressure (climate, rugged soil, unfriendly neighbors) has more virtue than one which does not; it has it because it has to have it; it can less afford to be vicious. Such peoples are more likely to meet transference with healthy reaction; on the other hand, they are also apt to be merely greedy, to make their mission war, and to die of inanition when there are no more worlds they can conquer.

Sixth, it does not seem possible that the multiple dialectic without grace can bring progress any further than the beginnings of reflex thought. The reason is that the transference of reflex thought involves the transference of major decline; in other words, that transference does not enable reflex thought to escape decline.

Accordingly, the fullness of time when Christ was born would seem to be that the multiple dialectic without grace had gone as far as it could.

(d) Single dialectic with grace

The principle of renaissance is essentially opposed to decline; acceptance of it, however, is a matter of free individual choice. Thus, the single dialectic with grace is not free from decline but it has a different progress and decline from the single dialectic without grace.

23 Lonergan is referring to a series of pamphlets (40 in total) published in five volumes with the general title *Studies in Comparative Religion* (London: Catholic Truth Society, [approx. 1935]). The general editor was Ernest Charles Messenger. Lonergan is probably working from memory, and seems to have mistaken the general title in his recall. Pamphlet 39 by E.C. Messenger is titled 'A Philosophy of Comparative Religion' (vol. 5). In volume 3, there are three pamphlets on Judaism: Pamphlet 17, 'Patriarchal and Mosaic Religion,' Pamphlet 18, 'The Religion of the Hebrew Prophets,' and Pamphlet 19, 'The Religion of Post-Exilic Judaism,' all three by J. M. Barton. Volume 4 includes Pamphlet 25, 'Medieval Christianity' by Christopher Dawson and Pamphlet 28, 'The Church and the Modern Age' by Christopher Hollis.

Its initial progress is deeper and more balanced, for its supreme interest is in the higher values. Thus it can carry cultural development far further than the dialectic without grace.

Its decline is longer delayed. For individuals to resist grace is not at once a social apostasy. For society to fall from grace is not at once for society to desert the natural law.

Its goal is not the simple animalization of man and atomization of society. Rather it tends to a disruption of society, its division into opposing camps in vital conflict. Christ came on earth to bring not peace but the sword [see Matthew 10.34]. Thus the syntheses and mysticisms of the modern world have their basic significance and their ultimate force in their anti-Catholicism. (Cf. Belloc, *Europe and the Faith*.)[24]

(e) Multiple dialectic with grace

It is to be observed that the 'new order' merges into a higher single dialectic of many phases the aggregate of social units it embraces. Thus the multiple dialectic with grace is not this higher single dialectic, but rather the place in the whole of history of this higher single dialectic.

Thus the questions of transference and reaction here belong to the science of missiology, where missiology is considered not as the concrete problems of the apostolate in particular countries but the larger questions of distributing and directing missionary effort over the globe. The issues a developed theory of history might examine would be the relative facility and the relative durability and value of conversion in the different stages of the single dialectic. Thus in the abstract a people in decline but with a future would seem the ideal from all points of view.

(f) Significance of history

The significance of history is a blend of the significance of its three elements: the progress of nature, the decline of sin, the renaissance of grace.

The progress of nature is the glory of the goodness of God.

The decline of sin is the glory of his majesty, that no flesh should glory in his sight.

24 Hilaire Belloc, *Europe and the Faith* (New York: Paulist Press, 1920).

The renaissance of grace is the glory of his transcendence. On earth it is the cross: the rest of history is the diluted epiphany of Calvary and the Mass. In heaven, it is the amazed exclamation in the instant of eternity, Holy, Holy, Holy!

8 Analytic Concept of History[1]

1 See above, p. 95, note 1. Lonergan's original manuscript is available in digital form on www.bernardlonergan.com at 71302DTE030. A version of this essay edited by Frederick E. Crowe appeared in *METHOD: Journal of Lonergan Studies* 11:1 (Spring 1993) 1–35. The current edition is in debt to Crowe's work and borrows from his notes. See p. 1 of Crowe's edition for his dating of the essay between midsummer of 1937 and fall of 1938. And see Shute, *Origins* 121–44.

2 This heading is not found in Lonergan's list of contents either here or at the beginning of section 3, but it does appear as a heading within that section. The addition here is editorial.

4 The three categories
  (a) Human actions fall into three categories.
  (b) This division is metaphysically ultimate.
  (c) Higher synthesis is impossible.
5 The ideal line of history
  (a) What is meant by an ideal line?
  (b) What is the ideal line of history?
  (c) What is the earthly task of man?
  (d) That there is progress
  (e) That this progress may be outlined from the nature of the human mind[3]
  (f) The nature of the human mind, inasmuch as we are concerned[4]
  (g) The three periods of history and their characteristics
6 Decline
  (a) The nature of decline
  (b) The goal of decline
  (c) The three forms of decline
  (d) Minor decline
  (e) Major decline
  (f) Compound decline
7 Renaissance
  (a) The essential character of renaissance
  (b) Characteristics of renaissance
  (c) Consequences of renaissance
8 The multiple dialectic
  (a) Single and multiple dialectic
  (b) Single dialectic without grace
  (c) Single dialectic with grace
  (d) Multiple dialectic without grace
  (e) Multiple dialectic with grace
  (f) Meaning of history

1 Analytic concepts

  (a) Concepts of apprehension and concepts of understanding
  (b) Analytic and synthetic acts of understanding

---

3 The manuscript shows three variant phrasings of this title: in the full table
   of contents, the table for section 5, and the text itself.
4 There is a similar variation in this title.

(c) Logical and real analysis
(d) Progress of understanding
(e) The analytic concept of history

(a) Concepts of apprehension and concepts of understanding[5]

By the concept of apprehension we know the object, what it is, what it is not; we do not understand it, know why it is what it is. The botanical definitions of flora would seem of this type.

By the concept of the understanding, in addition to knowing what the object is and what it is not, we also know what makes it what it is; and in this knowledge we have a premise to further knowledge. From the definition of a flower you can deduce nothing, save by what W.R. Thompson calls 'descending induction,'[6] which is either *petitio principii* or a guess. From the definition of the circle you deduce the properties of the circle.

(b) Analytic and synthetic acts of understanding

Any act of understanding is the apperceptive unity of a many: rather, any human act [of understanding], for God's is One of the One.

Now if the many be abstract terms, we have analytic understanding.

If the many be concrete, we have synthetic understanding.

Examples of the latter are, say, Christopher Dawson's historical essays, Newman's illative sense.[7] Examples of [the] former, infra.[8]

---

5 Crowe's note (2, p. 30) indicates that concepts of apprehension and concepts of understanding 'are related to the nominal and essential (or explanatory) definitions of later writings.' See, for example, Bernard Lonergan, *Insight: A Study of Human Understanding*, ed. Frederick E. Crowe and Robert M. Doran (Toronto: University of Toronto Press, 1992) 35–37.

6 W.R. Thompson, *Science and Common Sense: An Aristotelian Excursion* (London: Longmans Green & Co., 1937) 32. Thompson describes descending induction: 'a passing from a general proposition to a particular, from the plane of the intelligible to the plane of sensible things.' Crowe's note (3, p. 30) states, '… Thompson's *Science and Common Sense: An Aristotelian Excursion* … speaks of induction that goes from the particular to the general as an ascension, and of its reversal as a *descending induction* (p. 32); neither form of argument can avoid uncertainty, even though the descending induction is put into deductive form. For Lonergan's "begging of the question" [*petitio principii*] Thompson had "a surreptitious assumption" (p. 33).'

7 See above, p. 129, note 4.

8 See the three examples of analytic concepts in the next section, (c).

(c) Logical and real analysis

When the act of understanding is the unification of abstract terms, these terms may be a logical or a real multiplicity.

The essential definition of man, 'rational animal,' is a logical multiplicity, genus and difference.

The following analytic concepts are based upon real analysis.

The metaphysical concept of material reality as a compound of existence and essence, accident and substance, matter and form.

The chemist's concept of material things as compounds of elements.

The Newtonian analysis of planetary motion as a straight line modified by accelerations towards the sun and the other planets.

(d) Progress of understanding

Intellectus procedit a maius generali ad maius particulare; procedit per actus incompletos ad actum perfectum.[9]

First we understand things diagrammatically, in outline; we get the main point, the basic point of view; then we fill in the details.

(e) The analytic concept of history

It is an act of understanding: knowing why history is what it is.

It is based upon analysis, not synthesis: it does not proceed from historical fact to theory, but from abstract terms to the categories of any historical event.

Its analysis is real, not logical: nature, sin, and grace are not a logical but a real multiplicity.

Its real analysis is not of the static (being) but of the dynamic (action), and so its conclusions are not merely metaphysical categories as essence and existence but a causally and chronologically interrelated view, as the Newtonian astronomy.

Finally, the analytic concept of history is of maximum generality: we aim only at the fundamental and primordial understanding of history.

2 *History*

(a) History and historiography
(b) Material and formal objects of history
(c) The formal object of the analytic concept of history

9 See Thomas Aquinas, *Summa theologiae*, 1, q. 85, a. 3.

(a) [History and historiography]

Distinguish (i) history that is written, history books; call it historiography;
(ii) history that is written about.

(b) [Material and formal objects of history]

The material object of history is the aggregate of human thoughts, words,
and deeds.

The formal object of history is this aggregate placed in a perspective
by the historian's principle of selection. Now this principle of selection is
that 'an event is *historic* in the measure it influences human action.' Hence
we may simply say that history is the aggregate of human actions in their
causes. As such it is a science.

But it is to be noted that the historian considers the aggregate only by
considering the parts, that he finds his causes principally not without but
within the aggregate, and finally that effect is only a different aspect of
cause so that asking what are the effects of given actions is tantamount to
asking the cause of subsequent ones.

(c) [The formal object of the analytic concept of history]

The formal object of the analytic concept of history is to be obtained by
removing from the formal object of history all that is not subject to a
priori determination, *quoad nos*.

The formal object of history is the aggregate of human actions in their
causes (or effects). From this we remove the following elements.

First, because there is no science of the particular, we shall not be concerned
with 'Who did it?,' with persons or peoples, but solely with 'What is done?'

Second, because the action of the First Cause, though more excellent in
itself, is less known to us, we shall confine ourselves to secondary causes.
N.B. This will not exclude a hypothetical consideration of the supernatural virtues and the conditions of their emergence in history.

Third, among secondary causes we must distinguish essential and accidental, to omit the latter.

Among accidental causes are *actus hominis*[10] and 'acts of God' such as
plagues, famines, earthquakes, floods. We do not pretend to deny that such

10 See above, p. 98, note 5.

events may have the greatest historical importance (e.g., the Black Death); our position is that history is not essentially a succession of such events.

The essential causes of history are human wills, not in their immanent merits or demerits, but in their effective transience by which they influence others both directly and indirectly.

By direct influence we mean the influence exerted by one man upon others, whether it is convincing of what is true, persuading to what is right, indoctrinating with falsehood, conspiring to evil, or adding to all these the necessary use of force.

By indirect influence we mean the influence of the manmade environment, for instance, that of being born and brought up in Mayfair or in the jungle; also, the influence of the historical situation which past action created and present action has to face.

Fourth, in the essential causes of history we distinguish between those of formal and those of material import, that is, between vectors which give the magnitude and direction of forces and mere friction. The former is will exerted upon the manner of life; the latter is the will to live and to propagate.

Briefly, the formal object of the analytic concept of history is the *making and unmaking of man by man*.[11]

To the objection that the human will is free, that it is not subject to a priori determination, that therefore it cannot enter into our own view of the formal object of the analytic concept (see above, c), we answer that we have a method of outflanking this difficulty which will appear in due course.[12]

3 The dialectic

    (a) The nature of the dialectic
    (b) The existence of the dialectic
    (c) The subject of the dialectic
    (d) The form of the dialectic
    (e) Rates of the dialectic

(a) The nature of the dialectic

By the dialectic we do not mean Plato's orderly conversation, nor Hegel's expansion of concepts, nor Marx's fiction of an alternative to mechanical materialism.

11 In the typescript the words here italicized are all in upper-case letters.
12 See the treatment of solidarity below, pp. 160–61.

We do mean something like a series of experiments, a process of trial and error; yet not the formal experiment of the laboratory, for man is not so master of his fate; rather an inverted experiment, in which *objective reality molds the mind of man into conformity with itself by imposing upon him the penalty of ignorance, error, sin, and at the same time offering the rewards of knowledge, truth, righteousness.*

Suffice to note that objective reality does not mean merely material reality: it means all reality and especially Reality itself.

The illustration of the process is to be had from the microcosm: as the individual learns and develops so does mankind.

(b) The existence of the dialectic

The material object of history is an aggregate: if it is simply a many without any intelligible unity, there is no possibility of there being a dialectic. If there is some unity, then at least the dialectic is possible.

That the dialectic is possible follows from the solidarity of man.

What is this solidarity? Apart from the obvious biological fact, it may be summed up in the phrase: We make ourselves not out of ourselves but out of our environment (where 'environment' has the universality of the Ignatian *reliqua*).[13]

We make ourselves, for the will is free.

We do not make ourselves out of ourselves: *quidquid movetur ab alio movetur.*[14] The motion of action comes from outside us; the specification of action comes from outside us, though we may choose this specification in preference to that, or refuse any.

We make ourselves out of our environment: the physical environment that makes the geographical differentiations of men and manners and cultures; the social environment of the family and education, the race and tradition, the state and law.

Solidarity makes the dialectic possible. Is it actual?

The question is already answered. Man's freedom is limited. The will follows the intellect in truth, or obscures it to error, or deserts it to leave man an animal. The last is either sporadic and accidental and so of no concern to essential history, or it is based upon the second, the obscuration of the intellect. Now, whether men think rightly or wrongly, they

13 See above, p. 101, note 10.
14 See Thomas Aquinas, *Summa theologiae*, 1, q. 2, a. 3.

think in a herd. The apparent exception is genius, who however is not the fine flower of individuality but the product of the age and the instrument of the race in its progress. The illusory exception is acceptance by the herd of the liberal dogma of 'Think for yourself' along with all its implications.

(c) The subject of the dialectic

Strictly, the subject of the dialectic is any group united in time and place that think alike.

Practically, we may consider as the subject of the dialectic the social unit of tribe or state. The tribe or state creates a channel of mutual influence, and within it men both tend to agree and, when not so inclined, are forced to agree, at least to the extent of acting as though they did. Thus, in all public affairs and variously in private matters, the members of a social unit are ruled by a common way of thought. This is the dominant and the socially effective thought; it governs action; and all other, whatever be its future, is for the moment little more than mere thought.

But ideas have no frontiers. Thus, above the dialectics of single social units we may discern a 'multiple dialectic,' whose subject is humanity. It is constituted by the many dialectics of the different social units, in their interactions and their transferences from one unit to another.

(d) The form of the dialectic

We have already defined the dialectic as an inverted experiment in which objective reality molds the mind of man into conformity with itself.

The following observation will make this more precise.

Because the unity of the dialectic is the unity of thought that goes into action, it follows that this thought produces the social situation with its problems. If the thought is good, the problems will be small and few; thus the situation will require but slight modifications of previous thought and leave man opportunity to advance and develop. If, on the other hand, the thought is poor, then its concrete results will be manifestly evil and call for a new attitude of mind.

Taking the matter more largely, we may say that the dominant thought at any time arose from preceding situations; that its tendency is to transform the actual situation either by correction or by development; that the transformed situation will give rise to new thought, and this not merely to suggest it but to impose it by the threat of suffering or the promise of well-being.

(e) Rates of the dialectic

Roughly, we may distinguish three rates of the dialectic: normal, sluggish, and feverish. Normal defines itself. Sluggish would be the lack of response to the evils in the objective situation, whether this be from lack of intelligence or from fatalistic resignation or from the imprisonment of the individual in a straightjacket social scheme. Feverish would be excessive activity, and this from the intolerable pressure of objective evil or from unbalanced optimism or from the breakup of society.

From this difference of rate, it will be seen that when the dialectic is sluggish, essential history is at a standstill; when it is feverish, then essential history moves at a dizzy pace. Thus the dormant East will not exemplify our theory as does the history of the last four hundred years in Europe.

4 The three categories

(a) Human actions fall into three categories
(b) This division is metaphysically ultimate
(c) Higher synthesis is impossible

(a) Human actions fall into three categories

Man acts according to nature, contrary to nature, above nature.
The three categories are nature, sin, grace.

(b) [This division is metaphysically ultimate]

Action according to human nature is intelligible to man.
Action contrary to nature is unintelligible.
Action above nature is too intelligible for man.
But the intelligible, unintelligible, and too intelligible are metaphysically ultimate categories: they stand on the confines of our intelligence itself.
N.B. By stating that action contrary to nature is unintelligible, we do not mean that it is unknowable. Sin is a possible object of the judgment;

it is not a possible object of the understanding. For the understanding is the power by which we know why a thing is what it is: but sin of its very nature has no 'why it is what it is.' Sin admits no explanation: it is a desertion of reason, and so has no reason that is more than a pretense. Why did the angels sin? Why did Adam sin? There is no 'why.' We do not say there is a 'why' which we cannot know: we say there is no 'why' to be known. We do not say that God had not excellent reasons for permitting sin: so we do not evacuate the *mysterium iniquitatis*; indeed, we add another mystery, which, however, is not a mystery from excess of intelligibility but from lack of it. Hence, 'Nemo ex me scire quaerat, quod me nescire scio; nisi forte ut nescire discat, quod sciri non posse sciendum est.'[15]

(c) Higher synthesis is impossible

To posit a higher synthesis there must be the possibility of setting an antithesis against the thesis. But our thesis includes the intelligible to man, the unintelligible *simpliciter*, and the too intelligible for man. Outside these categories there is nothing, and so an antithesis is impossible.

5 *The ideal line of history*

   (a) What is meant by an ideal line?
   (b) What is the ideal line of history?
   (c) What is the earthly task of man?
   (d) That there is progress
   (e) That the progress may be determined from the nature of mind[16]
   (f) The nature of the mind of man, insofar as concerns us[17]
   (g) The three periods of history and their characteristics

(a) What is meant by an ideal line?

In mechanics the ideal line is drawn by Newton's first law: that a body continues to move in a straight line with uniform speed as long as no

15 See above, p. 105, note 15.
16 See above, p. 155, note 3.
17 See above, p. 155, note 4.

extrinsic force intervenes. It is the first approximation in the determination of every mechanical motion. And its value is undiminished by the fact that in this world of ours, the first law is absolutely impossible of actual verification.

Hence by an ideal line of history we mean the determination of the course of events that supplies the first approximation to any possible course of human history.

(b) What is the ideal line of history?

The ideal line of history is the history that would arise did all men under all conditions in all thoughts, words, and deeds obey the natural law, and this without the aid of grace.

It envisages, then, a state of pure nature, in which men as a matter of fact do not sin, though they are not destined to a supernatural end and do not need the *gratia sanans* that counteracts the wounds of original sin.

(c) What is the earthly task of man?

The proximate end of man is the making of man: giving him his body, the conditions of his life, the premotions to which he will respond in the fashioning of his soul.

Essentially, history is the making and unmaking and remaking of man: in the ideal line, we consider only the making of man by man.

(d) That there is progress

The earthly task of man is not a routine but a progress.

Homo est in genere intelligibilium ut potentia; intellectus procedit per actus incompletos ad actum perfectum.[18]

But this gradual actuation of man's intellectual potency is the achievement not of the individual, nor of a few generations, but of mankind in all places and through all time. What the angel, a species to himself, attains instantaneously in *aevum*, an indefinitely distended point, that man achieves in time, the whole time of his earthly existence.

18 See Thomas Aquinas, *Summa theologiae*, 1, q. 87, a. 1; 1, q. 85, a. 3.

(e) That the course of human progress may be determined from the nature of the human mind [19]

The instrument of human progress is the mind of man. If, then, the mind of man is such that some things must be known first and others later, an analysis of mind will reveal the outlines of progress.

(f) The nature of the mind of man, insofar as concerns us [20]

The human intellect is a conscious potency conditioned by sense.

Insofar as it is a conscious potency, there are two types of intellectual operation: spontaneous and reflex.

Since the reflex use of intellect presupposes the discovery of the canons of thought and the methods of investigation, it follows that there is first a spontaneous period of thought and second a period of reflex thought.

Next, inasmuch as the human intellect is conditioned by experience we may roughly distinguish two fields of knowledge.

First, there is the philosophic field, in which thought depends upon the mere fact of experience (general metaphysic) or upon its broad and manifest characters (cosmology, rational psychology, ethics).

Second, there is the scientific field, in which thought depends not upon experience in general nor upon its generalities but upon details of experience observed with the greatest care and accuracy.

Finally, roughly corresponding to these two fields of knowledge are two manners or methods of thought: deductive from the general to the particular; inductive from the particular to the general.

Now, on the one hand, deductive thought proceeds in a straight line of development, while on the other, inductive thought proceeds in a series of revolutions from theses through antitheses to higher syntheses.

Deductive thought proceeds in a straight line, for its progress is simply a matter of greater refinement and accuracy. There is an exception to this rule, for deductive thought does suffer revolutionary progress until it finds its fundamental terms and principles of maximum generality: there were philosophers before Aristotle, and, more interesting, modern mathematics has been undergoing revolutions not because mathematics is not

19 See above, p. 155, note 3.
20 See above, p. 155, note 4.

a deductive science but because the mathematicians have been generalizing their concepts of number and space.

Inductive thought proceeds by thesis, antithesis, and higher synthesis. This follows from the nature of the understanding, the intellectual light that reveals the one in the many. For per se *intellectus est infallibilis*; but de facto understanding is of things not as they are in themselves but as they are apprehended by us. The initial understanding of the thesis is true of the facts as they are known, but not all are known; further knowledge will give the antithesis, and further understanding the higher synthesis.

Thus, there are two ways of being certain of one's understanding: the first is philosophic and excludes the possibility of higher synthesis; the second is full knowledge of the facts, Newman's real apprehension. Granted a real apprehension and an understanding of what is apprehended, we may be certain: for per se *intellectus est infallibilis*, while the real apprehension excludes the possibility of antithetical fact arising.

(g) The three periods of history and their characteristics

First, from the distinction of spontaneous and reflex thought, we have three periods of history: (1) spontaneous history and spontaneous thought; (2) spontaneous history and reflex thought; (3) reflex history and reflex thought.

The first period is from the beginning to the discoveries of philosophy and science.

The second period is from these discoveries to the social application of philosophy and science to human life in its essential task: the making of man.

The third is society dominated by the consciousness of its historic mission: the making or unmaking of man.

We would note that the second period does not end with the writing of Plato's *Republic*, nor even with the medieval application of philosophy to society, but rather with the social passion for an ideal republic that marked the French Revolution, the nineteenth-century liberals, the modern communists, and the promised Kingship of Christ through Catholic Action and missiology. The 'class consciousness' advocated by the communists is perhaps the clearest expression of the transition from reflex thought to reflex history.

Second, from the distinction of philosophic and scientific, deductive and inductive thought, we may distinguish two levels of thought in each of the three periods. Thus:[21]

(1) Spontaneous thought and history
   Deductive field: popular religion and morality
   Inductive field: agriculture, mechanical arts
   economic and political structures
   fine arts, humanism
   discovery of philosophy and science
(2) Reflex thought but spontaneous history
   Deductive field: religion and morality on philosophic basis
   Inductive field: applied science, international law (*ius gentium*)
   enlightenment
   theories of history
(3) Reflex thought and history
   Deductive field: the 'general line' of history philosophically determined (cf. Stalin's general line)[22]
   Inductive field: edification of world state
   Third, to this table we may add certain general norms.

(1) Progress is from the spontaneous social unit of tribe or race to the reflex social unit of the state.
(2) The development of humanistic culture presupposes large-scale agriculture; its universalization presupposes applied science: priority of the economic as a condition.
(3) The tendency of progress is to remove man from his dependence upon nature to dependence upon the social structure, to substitute state for kinship.
(4) The greater the progress, the greater the differentiation of occupation, the more complex the social structure, and the wider its extent: for man progresses by intellect's domination over matter; but this

---

21 Inserted by hand in the line of space after 'Thus,' and referring perhaps to the three-part schema that follows in the text, is this notation: 'Note: thesis not wrong but incomplete; perhaps wrong fundamentally. *Spiritual harm.*'
22 See above, p. 139, note 12.

domination is that of the universal over the many: its exploitation, hierarchy.[23] (Progress as intellectual.)[24]

(5) Man must not permit himself to be led by the nose by this progress: the result would be wonderfully intelligible but not human. Man has an intellect, but he is not an intellect. Virtue is in the mean, even the virtue of progress. ([Progress] as human.)

6 Decline

(a) The nature of decline
(b) The goal of decline
(c) The three forms of decline
(d) Minor decline
(e) Major decline
(f) Compound decline

(a) [The nature of decline]

We defined the ideal line as the constant and complete observance of the natural law. Decline is the deviation from the ideal line that is consequent to nonobservance.

It is to be noted that we deal not with a new line but with a deviation from the line already established. Though in this outline we merely indicate the abstract form of decline, it is not to be inferred that we have left over a problem of relating decline with the ideal line but only of making the theory of decline more full and detailed.

(b) [The goal of decline]

The goal of decline is contained in its principle, sin. Sin is the repudiation of reason in a particular act. Decline is the social rule of sin, its gradual

---

23 Lonergan added the last three words by hand; their meaning is revealed in the previous entry, 'Analytic Concept of History, in Blurred Outline,' above, p. 140: 'The power of intellect is the domination of the universal over the material many; its exploitation is hierarchy.'

24 Next to this paragraph (4) are the handwritten words 'progress as intellectual,' while next to paragraph (5) we have '[Progress] as human.' In each case the reference seems to be to the whole paragraph.

domination of the dialectic and the minds of men dependent upon this dialectic because of their solidarity. Thus the goal of decline is the unchaining of the animal, with intellect so far from being master that it is the slave of instinct and passion.

Plainly this triumph of the beast differs in the three periods: the degenerate savage Nero and the New Paganism of Germany differ vastly; but they would seem to be triumphs of the beast on different levels of history.

(c) [The three forms of decline]

The three forms of decline, minor and major and compound, are distinguished as follows.

Minor is the effect of sin in the inductive field of thought.

Major is the effect of sin in the deductive field of thought.

Compound is the combination and interaction of both together.

(d) [Minor decline]

Practical progress or social improvement proceeds by the laws of inductive thought: its theses indeed are not simply false, else they could hardly begin to function; but they are incomplete, as classical education is incomplete and so finds an antithesis in the modern side. Now the new syntheses of progressive understanding have three disadvantages:

(1) it is not clear that they offer the better, for concrete issues are complex;

(2) it is certain they threaten the liquidation of what is tried and established, and so they meet with the inevitable bias and opposition of the vested interests;

(3) in most cases they contain an element of risk and demand the spirit that contemns the sheltered life – insured from tip to toe – and so meet with the condemnation of all whose wisdom is more lack of courage than penetration of intellect.

Thus the mere fact of progress produces social tension, and every little boy or girl is born liberal or conservative. But minor decline begins with sin.

Radix omnium malorum cupiditas.

Self-interest is never enlightened because it is never objective: it sees the universe with the 'ego' at the center, but the 'ego' of the individual or the class or the nation is not the center.

This bias of practical thought transforms the distinction of those who govern and those who are governed into a distinction between the privileged and the depressed. The latter distinction in time becomes an abyss: its mechanism would seem as follows. Insensibly the privileged find the solution to the antitheses of their own well-being and progress. Too easily they pronounce nonexistent or insoluble the antitheses that militate against the well-being of the depressed.

Thus it is that with the course of time, the privileged enjoy a rapid but narrowly extended expansion of progress, and meanwhile the depressed are not merely left behind but more or less degraded by the set of palliatives invented and applied to prevent their envy bursting into the flame of anger and revolution. The total result is an objective disorder: both the progress of the few and the backwardness of the many are distorted; the former by its unnatural exclusiveness, the latter by the senseless palliatives. And this distortion is not merely some abstract grievance waiting on mere good will and polite words to be set right: it is the concrete and almost irradicable form of achievements, institutions, habits, customs, mentalities, characters.

So much for minor decline.

(e) Major decline

The essence of major decline is sin on principle. When men sin against their consciences, their sins are exceptions to a rule that is recognized and real. When they deform their consciences, sin from being the exception to the law becomes the law itself. This erection of sin into a law of action is the essence of major decline.

There are three elements in the deformation of the conscience.

First, there is the tendency to self-justification. The consciousness of man seeks the harmony of unity and consistency: by his actions man is sinful; therefore he will either reform his actions by doing penance or he will reform his conscience by denying sin to be sin. See Isaias 5.20–23.[25]

25 See above, p. 141, note 14.

Second, there is the objective foundation that gives this lie in the soul its color of truth. Men sin, and the effects of their sins are concrete and real and objective. They set a dilemma to the just man: for if he acknowledges the *fait accompli* he cooperates with injustice; and if he refuses to acknowledge it, then he lives in an imaginary world and cannot cope with the real one. But to the unjust such situations are but proof that justice is injustice, that good is evil and evil good, that right is wrong and wrong right.

Third, as a combination and generalization of the preceding two: there is the discrediting of deductive knowledge. Socrates can demonstrate to his heart's content: it is obvious he is wrong, and that's all about it (cf. *Gorgias*).[26] Or in the period of reflex thought, philosophy turns from the contemplation of truth to the problem, Why are all the philosophers wrong?[27]

Thus the major decline is the gradual procession, from sins to sins on principle, and from sins on principle to the dethronement of reason and the emancipation of the beast (see Nabuchodonosor [*sic*], Apocalypse).[28]

But major decline may be viewed from another standpoint: that of the understanding. The yielding of deductive thought is marked by an invasion of understanding into the deductive field. The inertia of a culture makes for the preservation of all the good that can be saved at each stage of the wrecking process. Thus we have a series of *lower syntheses*. In the spontaneous period this is expressed by the gradual corruption of the gods. In the reflex period we have Christendom, Protestantism, rationalism, liberalism, naturalism, communism, nationalism.[29]

---

26 Crowe comments, p. 33, note 39, 'The reference does not seem to be to any particular exchange in the *Gorgias* but to the general difficulty Socrates has in dialogue with Gorgias, Polus, and Callicles.' But see the reference to the *Gorgias* above, in a similar context, at p. 108.

27 See above, p. 113.

28 Crowe suggests, p. 33, note 40, 'The first reference may be to Daniel 4.33, where it is said of Nebuchadnezzar: "He was driven away from human society, ate grass like oxen, and his body was bathed with the dew of heaven, until his hair grew as long as eagles' feathers and his nails became like birds' claws" (NRSV). The second reference may be to Revelation 13.2: "And the beast that I saw was like a leopard, its feet were like a bear's, and its mouth was like a lion's mouth. And the dragon gave it his power and his throne and great authority" (NRSV).'

29 Handwritten below this paragraph: 'Each its "mysticism" propaganda persecution (you would think Protestants never used the torture chamber nor liberals the guillotine).'

(f) Compound decline

Both the major accelerates the minor and vice versa.

The major accelerates the minor. It deprives science – notably, economics – and practical thought of the guidance of the first principles of religion and morality. Of itself the minor tends to disorder; coupled with the major its goal is an unintelligible chaos. For sin is unintelligible: action guided by sin results in the unintelligible – no mere antithesis to be easily swallowed by some higher synthesis but an indigestible morsel refractory to all intellect that can be solved only by liquidation.

On the other hand, the minor accelerates the major, inasmuch as it supplies the real mechanism for the imposition of the successive lower syntheses. The tension between liberal and conservative, the opposition between privileged and depressed, take on a philosophic significance when the disputes engendered by the major decline are made the sponsors of slogans for rival cupidities and hatreds. The goddess Reason is enthroned amidst blasphemy and bloodshed. Liberalism gains the fascination of a snake by its polite contempt for religion. The proletariat attains consciousness by militant atheism.

Nor are we to overlook, in the combination of major and minor decline, a third element that is prior to both: progress. The French Revolution rid the world of feudal survivals. The liberal revolution was founded upon an amazing industrial advance. Communism not only excites rabid nationalism but does so because it would transcend the tribes.

7 Renaissance

(a) The essential character of renaissance
(b) Characteristics of renaissance
(c) Consequences of renaissance

(a) The essential character of renaissance

Progress is the thesis of nature; decline the antithesis of sin; the higher synthesis of these two necessarily lies beyond the confines of this world and the intellect of man. It is not the mind of man that can make issue with the unintelligibility of sin and the distortion and dethronement of the mind itself.

Hence the essential character of renaissance is that it presupposes a transcendence of humanity, the emergence of a 'new' order.

(Compare truth and error in Trotskyist 'continual revolution.')[30]

(b) Characteristics of renaissance

What transcends man is to man as man is to the beast, the beast to the plant, the plant to the nonadaptive element.

From this follow the four characteristics of renaissance, the basic principles of a 'higher criticism' to replace the Hegelian.

First, the new order transcends man: therefore, it would be to man mystery; it would be to his understanding as his understanding is to the brute; *ta epekeina*.

Second, the new order would be knowable: man knows being, and outside being there is nothing. But because of the lack of understanding, this knowledge would be as the scientist's of empirical law.[31]

Third, man could not raise himself into the new order: nothing can transcend itself.

Fourth, in the new order, man's nature would not be negated but included in a higher synthesis. This, on analogy: man transcends but does not negate the orders beneath him; as a mass of matter, he is subject to the laws of mechanics; as living, he is subject to the laws of cellular development and decay; as sentient, he has the perceptions and appetites of the brute.

Hence, in the new order we would still have life under social conditions to an individualist end; the acceptance of the new order and life in it would be rational, and so be rationally acceptable (miracles) and humanly livable (authority).[32]

---

30 See above, p. 117 and note 34.
31 Handwritten at the end of this paragraph: 'not completely so.'
32 See above, 'Analytic Concept of History, in Blurred Outline,' p. 147: 'acceptance of the new order must be rational, and so evidence of its emergence must be provided (miracles)'; p. 148: 'against the successive ambiguities of the dialectic ... the new order will set a living authority providentially infallible ... against the dethronement of reason the new order will present its own rigorous and all-embracing rationalism under the higher synthesis of faith and authority.'

(c) Consequences of renaissance

We have envisaged the new order as the higher synthesis of progress and decline. Hence it will restore progress and offset decline.

To offset decline, the new order must attack major decline at its root: against self-justification it will set penance, against the objective unintelligibility and chaos it will set justice-transcending charity, against the discrediting of reason it will set faith. Again, against minor decline the new order must introduce what will compensate for the unbalance and bias of egoism: against cupidity, poverty of spirit; against revolution, obedience; against the beast, chastity.

To restore progress, the new order must restore ordered freedom: the order which holds the balance between the fields of reason and understanding, philosophy and science; the freedom that is the *autoliberazione* of the self-renouncing will; the ordered freedom in which all individuals find their own place of themselves, and all conspire for that infinitely nuanced 'better' that is the goal of progress, but can be known only by the work of all intelligences each in its own field, that can be attained only by individuals bearing the risks that each advance involves. Etc., etc.

8 The multiple dialectic

(a) Single and multiple dialectic

The single dialectic is, as we have seen, the succession of situation, thought, action, new situation, new thought, etc., within the social unit.

The multiple dialectic is the synthetic unity of the aggregate of single dialectics: it is this aggregate in their solidarity and differences, their transferences and reactions.

(b) Single dialectic without grace

Progress is of nature. Decline is the cumulative effect of sin. Hence it follows that the course of the history of the social unit, uninfluenced by grace,[33] is an initial progress that gradually is submerged in the mounting flood of sin. Further, this curve – first ascending, then

---

33 The Crowe edition, p. 26, has 'influenced by grace,' which is clearly a typist's error.

descending – is accentuated by the priority of the economic over the cultural: to labor for economic improvement is easy; to sacrifice for the impalpable benefits of culture is difficult. Thus the course of the history of the social unit in the case we are considering is: first, economic development; second, a certain measure of cultural advance; third, the animalization of man on the higher level of his achievement. (Compare Spengler's theory.)[34]

(c) Single dialectic with grace

The 'new order' eliminates the possibility of major decline within its own frontiers.

In the measure in which the evangelical counsels are embraced by an elite and their spirit observed by all, the 'new order' excludes the possibility of minor decline.

But adherence to the new order is a matter of free individual choice: hence the insertion of grace into the dialectic tends in the long run to disrupt the social unit. 'I have come on earth to bring not peace but the sword' [Matthew 10.34]. In a word, the 'vessels of wrath' [Romans 9.22] will find in the constraints of the new order not the guarantee of the stability of their initial progress but a hindrance to its expansion; they will find in the disproportion between the profession and the practice of the counsels an occasion for rebellion, and so open the door to major decline; and in major decline, the successive lower syntheses will be all the more violently asserted and vigorously brought into execution because of the presence of opposition.

The disruption that follows from grace must be distinguished from the atomization, the *Zersplitterung*, that follows from decline. Grace divides society into two opposing camps in vital conflict: it is the Socratic gadfly. Decline reduces man to the animal level, the stagnation of the sluggish dialectic. All the anti-Catholic syntheses and 'mysticisms' of the modern world have their significance and their force in their anti-Catholicism ultimately.

(Compare Donoso Cortés: Blood must flow: the only question is whether it flow in love or hatred.)[35]

34 See above, p. 149, note 22.
35 See above, p. 61 and note 35.

(d) Multiple dialectic without grace

The transition from the single dialectics to the multiple may best be made by considering transference and reaction.

Transference is the importation by a social unit of the achievements or the miseries of another.[36]

It is spatial when the units are contemporary; it is temporal when one unit inherits from another now in decay.

Reaction commonly denotes opposition to progress or decline within the social unit: here we use it to denote opposition to importation. We distinguish healthy and unhealthy reaction: healthy is opposition to the importation of foreign decadence; unhealthy is opposition to the importation of foreign progress.

The synthetic unity of the multiple dialectic without grace is:

Transference with healthy reaction results in the continuity of human progress despite the fact that each progressive social unity in turn succumbs to decline.

Transference without healthy reaction universalizes decline: it makes the backward people *brûler l'étape*[37] in the downward course of decline. Russia under the Soviets expiates the sins of the West. Native tribes learn the sins without emulating the achievements of the modern world. (Wars, conquest, white man's burden.)

(e) Multiple dialectic with grace

First consider the single dialectics with grace. These will be either in the initial stage of progress or the later stage of disruption. In the former case, the different social units will be united in a superstate, Christendom, and will act as one, more or less, against what is alien to them, Crusades. Again, as long as major decline is avoided, then no matter what the minor decline in any unit, there will remain the seeds of renaissance, of a second spring: the vitality of the West, rising out of the ruins of the Roman Empire and, despite continual lapses into minor decline, steadily advancing to achievement hitherto unattained.

36 In the space at the end of this line Lonergan wrote 'Formal Real (migration; conquest).' See above, p. 150: 'Transference is real or formal: real in the cases of migration and conquest; formal in the case of imitation – importation of ideas.'
37 'proceed rapidly.' See above, p. 150.

If on the other hand the social units are tending to disruption we would seem threatened with the persecutions and wars of the Apocalypse.

Finally, the relations between the dialectics with grace and those without form the subject matter of missiology.

(f) Meaning of history

The meaning of history is the relation of its three elements, progress, sin, and grace, to the First Cause and Last End.

Progress expresses the goodness of God, to whom all glory from all the multitudinous golden hearts in the world.

Sin is the wickedness of man, and decline 'that no flesh should glory in his sight' [1 Corinthians 1.29].

Grace is the higher synthesis of both in God's transcendence: on earth it is the cross, for Christ lived only till he was big enough to be crucified, and the rest of history is but a dilution of that expression of the value of man; but in heaven it is an exceeding weight of glory [2 Corinthians 4.17], when amazed and awed by the Infinite we exclaim in the one instant of eternity the one word, Holy, Holy, Holy!

Latin and Greek Words and Phrases

actu agere: actually to act

actus hominis: act of a human being (that may have no moral significance)

actus humanus: act of a human being that involves intellect and will

actus limitatur per potentiam: act is limited by potency

agere sequitur esse: action follows being, that is, something acts in accord
   with what it is

alter Christus: other Christ

amicus amat amicos amici: a friend loves the friends of one's friend

anakephalaiōsis: gathering together, restoration

analogice divinum qua divinum: analogically divine as divine

anēr pneumatikos: spiritual man

anēr psychikos: soulful man; Lonergan's meaning is 'merely natural
   man'

anēr sarkikos: fleshly man

anthropos pneumatikos: spiritual person

anthropos psykhikos: soulful person/natural person

anthropos sarkikos: fleshly person

appetitus rationalis [or *naturalis*] *sequens formam intellectus*: rational [natu-
   ral] inclination following the form of [that is, presented by] intellect

bonum hominis est secundum rationem esse: the human good consists in
   being according to reason

Carthago non delenda: Carthage is not to be destroyed

causa secunda et instrumentalis: a secondary, instrumental cause

Christiani ad leones: Christians to the lions

coepit veritas, simul atque apparuit, inimica esse: The first reaction to truth
 is hatred. The moment it appears, it is treated as an enemy.
contra rationem: against reason
corruptio optimi pessima: the corruption of the best is the worst of all
delicta quis intelliget? But who can detect their errors? (Psalm 19.12)
depositum fidei: deposit of the faith
divinorum operum omnium divinissimum Deo cooperari in salvatione ani-
 marum: the most divine of all acts is to cooperate with God in the
 salvation of souls
doctor invincibilis: invincible teacher
energeia: act/activity/actuation/dynamism
energeia est actus entis in actu inquantum huiusmodi: activity is the act of a
 being in act insofar as it is in act
esse absoluto/absolutum: absolute existence
esse relativum: relative existence
est aut non est: it is or it is not
generatio proprie dicta: generation properly so called
gratia sanans: healing grace
hē hagia Sophia: holy Wisdom
homo est in genere intelligibilium ut potentia; intellectus procedit per actus
 incompletos ad actum perfectum: man is in potency with respect to
 (in the genus of) intelligible things; the intellect proceeds through
 incomplete acts to a perfect act
homologoumenōs tē phusei zēn: in harmony with nature
homoousios: consubstantial
impavidum ferient ruinae: the ruins strike him undaunted (Horace)
inclinatio naturalis: natural inclination
indivisum in se et divisum a quolibet alio: undivided in itself and divided
 (distinct) from anything else
in genere intelligibilium ut actus: in act with respect to (in the genus of)
 intelligible things
in genere intelligibilium ut potentia: in potency with respect to (in the
 genus of) intelligible things
intellectus a magis generali ad magis particulare procedit: the intellect proceeds from the more general to the more particular
intellectus est infallibilis: intellect is infallible
intellectus procedit a maius generali ad maius particulare, per actus
 incompletos ad actum perfectum: the intellect proceeds from the
 general to the more particular, through incomplete acts to a perfect (complete) act

invicta schola nominalium: unconquered school of nominalists

ius gentium: the law of the nations

materia propter formam: matter has its end in form

motus est actus entis in potentia inquantum huiusmodi: motion is the act of a being in potency insofar as it is in potency

mutatis mutandis: the necessary changes having been made

mysterium iniquitatis: mystery of iniquity

nemo dat quod non habet: no one gives what one does not have

nemo repente summus: no one becomes very good suddenly

nihil sanctum: nothing is holy

non-ens: non-being

obiectum adaequatum et obiectum proportionatum: adequate object and proportionate object

odio humani generis convicti sunt: they were convicted for hatred of the human race.

odium fidei: hatred for the faith

odium humani generis: hatred for the human race

ordo cum tranquillitate: order with tranquility

pacificans omnia: reconciling all things and making peace (Colossians 1.20); literally, pacifying everything

pantōn anakephalaiōsis: restoration/gathering together of all things

per mortem ad vitam: through death to life

per se nota quoad se: self-evident in itself

petitio principii: begging the question

philosophia perennis: perennial philosophy

plerōma: fullness

pluvia defit, causa Christiani: when drought comes it is due to the Christians

posse agere: to be able to act, to be in potency to act

potentia est propter actum: potency is for (has its end in) act

primogenitus ex mortuis: firstborn from the dead

primum agens: first agent

principium intrinsecum actionis talis: intrinsic principle of such an action

qua tale: as such

quae sunt eadem uni tertio sunt eadem inter se: those things that are equal to a third thing are equal to each other

quidquid movetur ab alio movetur: whatever is moved is moved by something else

quidquid recipitur recipitur ad modum recipientis: whatever is received is received in accord with the mode of the receiver

quo quid est quod est: that by which something is what it is

quoad id quod est: in regard to what something is

quoad modum: in its mode

quoad modum quo est: in regard to the way something is

quoad nos: for us

quoad se: in itself

quoad substantiam: in its substance

radix omnium malorum cupiditas: the root of all evils is greed

ratio intelligibilis: intelligible nature, i.e., ground of intelligibility or
  meaning

ratio mali: aspect of evil

ratio philosophica: philosophical reason

ratio theologica: theological reason

ratione essentiae: by reason of essence

ratione materiae quantitate signatae: by reason of quantitatively desig-
  nated matter

ratione suppositi: by reason of the supposit

rationes formales: formal reasons/aspects

reliqua: the remainder; here used to refer to Ignatius Loyola's 'the
  other things on the face of the earth'

sanguis martyrum, semen ecclesiae: the blood of martyrs is the seed of the
  church

Sapientia manifestanda: Wisdom to be made manifest

secundum quid: in a qualified way

simpliciter: absolutely, without qualification

singuli autem alter alterius membra: individually members of one another

spiratio: spiration

spoliatus gratuitis, vulneratus in naturalibus: deprived of the supernatural
  gifts, wounded in nature

ta epekeina: the parts beyond

taedium vitae: the weariness of life

ultimum cur: ultimate why

unum in se et diversum a quolibet alio: one in itself and different from
  anything else

Verbum Divinum: Divine Word

vetera novis augere et perficere: to augment and complete the old with
  the new

voluntas non movetur nisi a dictamine rationis: the will is moved only by a
  dictate of reason

Biblical Texts

Index

Act: and imitation of divine essence, 40; imperfect/incomplete a., 9, 39 n. 2, 44–45, 46, 47, 55, 56, 59, 66, 69, 70; perfect a., 9, 39 n. 2, 44–45, 66; and potency, 9, 34, 39 n. 2, 40, 44, 45, 52, 77; and pure reality, 77

Action(s): a. of Spirit, 123; and actual grace, 29; causes of human a., 98; and dialectic, 103, 133, 135, 149, 174; direct and indirect a., 134; diversification of human a. and progress of intellect, 136–37; division of human a. (according to nature, contrary to nature, above nature), 96, 135, 162; external human a., *see* External human activity/action; first cause of human a., 98; human a. always predetermined to either rational or irrational, 7; human a. and human nature, 7–8, 62, 104–105, 135, 162; human a. governed by thought, 83, 84; human a. as intelligible to us, unintelligible, or too intelligible, 105; internal/immanent a. and external/transient a., 7; and material and formal objects of

history, 130–31, 158; and necessity of supernatural, 25; secondary causes of human a. essential and accidental, 98; and sin, 85–88, 113, 170, 172; solidarity of human a., 100; three categories of human a. (according to nature, contrary to nature, above nature), 96, 104–105, 162; three elements/causes in a. of individual merge in one a., 6; and transformation of data, 84–85; and transmission of premotion from first agent, 71; unity of human a./operation, 7, 10, 26, 29, 31, 34, 36, 68

Actus humanus: and *actus hominis*, 98 & n. 5, 99, 158, 179

Adam: first and second A., 27, 29, 36, 41, 54–55, 61–62, 71–73, 92; and intellectual advance, 67, 91

Aeterni Patris, 56

Aevum, 9, 45, 67, 133, 164

Alexander, 15

Anakephalaiōsis: as integration, restoration, 29, 39 n. 3, 62, 73, 179, 181; and premotion, 41

Analogy: of human and divine, 52–53

Analysis: logical, real, static, dynamic a., 129

Anēr/anthropos sarkikos, psychikos, pneumatikos, 30–31, 53, 66, 73, 79, 179

Angel: as individual, 52, 62, 73, 77, 100, 164; sin of, 62, 63, 73, 104, 135, 163

Angelic intellect, 9, 34, 45, 67, 100, 133, 164

Anticlericalism, 33, 125

Antipopes, 18, 20, 25, 51

Apprehension: a. real and distorted, and understanding, 108; concepts of, 127, 128, 154, 155, 156 & n. 5; Newman's real a., 109, 138, 166

Aquinas, Thomas, 9, 30, 33, 40, 44, 51 & n. 21, 56 & n. 26, 65 n. 2, 70 n. 13, 78. Works cited: *Summa theologiae*, 7 n. 6, 39 n. 2, 67 n. 6, 89 n. 5, 98 n. 5, 100 n. 8–9, 106 n. 20, 129 n. 5, 157 n. 9, 160 n. 14, 164 n. 18; *Super II Sententiarum*, 26 n. 26

Aristotle, 11, 16, 17, 33, 56, 67, 74, 86, 108, 137, 165

Armament manufacture, 24

Atomization: of humanity/society, 45, 47, 48, 58, 59, 116, 152, 175

Augustine, 42 n. 12, 45 n. 15, 49, 51, 71 n. 18, 105 n. 15, 116 & n. 33

Autoliberazione, 120, 140, 174

Automatic: a. cultural expansion from Dark Age to present, 11, 17; a. progress, 19; a. stage in history/progress, 11

Belloc, H., 108 & n. 22, 144 n. 17, 152 & n. 24

Bias: b. of practical thought, 111 & n. 27, 142, 170; egocentric b., 107, 142–43, 174; and vested interests, 169

Bolshevism, 18, 19, 20, 23, 24, 25, 30, 57, 63

Bourgeois, 111, 116, 117, 143

Brown, Patrick, 107 n. 21

Buddha: *see* Gotama/Buddha

Bureaucracy, 13, 117

Caesaropapism, 69

Capitalism/capitalists: and communism, 32, 46, 69

Catholic Action, 39, 57, 82, 94, 126, 139, 166

Catholic development: peculiarities of, and social order, 33

Causality: historical c. of Christ, 122 n. 38

Causation: historical c., 41, 43

Cause(s): accidental and essential c. of history/human action, 96, 98, 99, 115, 131–32, 158–59; c. of conformation of theory to bad practice, 144; c. of decline, 113, 119, 148; c. of deformation of conscience, 143; c. of error, 68; c. of good, 35; c. of revolutions, 112; chain of c., 41; Christ as formal and efficient c., 61; and definition of history, 131, 148, 158; first c. and meaning of history, 177; first c. and secondary c. of human action/history, 98, 131; formal and efficient c. of charity, 41; idea as formal c. needs efficient c. in will, 58; instrumental c. and human action, 41, 49, 50, 53, 54, 68, 72, 74–75; material, formal, and efficient c. of human action, 6; no c. of sin, 51; no change in c., 50–51 n. 21; principal c., 49–50, 72, 74–75

Chamberlain, H.S., 57 n. 29

Change: and bureaucracy, 13; flow of c. and human action, 6; and history, 85; and ideas/thought, 44, 102; no

c. in cause, 50–51 n. 21; three kinds
of, 31–32

Charity: and Catholic Action, 126; as
counterpiece/solution to evil, 37,
60, 70, 73, 119, 148, 174; efficient
cause of, 41; formal cause of, 41;
and justice, 88, 148, 174; and
objective evil; and personality, 71;
and sanctifying grace, 60 and n. 34;
and self–interest, 107; and unity of
humanity, 74

Chemistry: and analytic concepts, 96,
129; and progress/decline, 115

Christ: and actual grace, 29; assimilation to, 122, 124, 126; and dogma,
55, 57, 59; as first mover of a new
order, 28; as formal cause of charity,
41; as formal and efficient cause and
end of universe, 61; kingship of, 37
& n. 41, 39, 57, 59, 139, 166; mystical body of, *see* Mystical body; as
object for love of will, 60; as *pantōn
anakephalaiōsis*, 58–61; Pauline
conception of C. and creation, 54;
and peace, 59, 73; and philosophy,
55; and Plato's philosopher king,
34, 59; premotion of/consequent
to C., 29, 35, 41, 55, 73, 122; and
progress, 36; and redemption, 92;
as second Adam, 36, 54–55, 72–73,
74, 92; and synthetic view of convergence, 40; and unity of human
action, 29

Christianity: and dialectic, 30; and
schism, 129; and Scholastic science,
18; at once symbol and higher
control, 20

Church: and automatic cultural expansion, 17–18; and Bolshevism, 19, 57,
63; and confession, 22, 60, 70; and
conscience, 22; decline in c., 125; and
dialectic, 22; and heresy, 63, 125; and

influence on external action, 8; as
instrumental cause, 54, 72; intellectualist position of c., 56; and internal
act of will, 5, 8; and international
society, 110; magisterium of c., 22;
and philosophy, 30, 34; and premotions from Christ, 122; progress of
c., 125–26; and rationalization of sin,
59, 70; and schism, 129; and scientific sociology and missiology, 30; and
state, 5, 20, 21–22, 63;

Class: c. consciousness, 139, 166; c.
egoism, 111, 170; c. spirit, 120; c.
war, 142

Classical education, 109, 140

Communism: and church and liberalism, 32, 33; and class, 139, 142,
166; as consequent of capitalist
exploitation and oppression, 46;
and decline, 86, 144, 171, 172; and
dialectic of sin, 82; dogma of c., 57;
marital c. (Plato), 16; and mysticism
of revolution, 115; and rationalism,
22; and reflex history, 166; and
religion, 20, 46, 69

Concept(s): analytic c., 95, 96–97,
127, 154, 155–57 (*see also* History:
analytic concept of); c. of apprehension, 127, 154, 156; and symbol,
15–16, 20; c. of understanding, 127,
128–29, 154, 156

Concupiscence, 46, 55, 58, 91

Confession: auricular c., 22, 60, 70, 88

Confucius, 44

Conscience: bourgeois c., 143; and
church, 22; deformation of, 22,
113–14, 141, 142, 143, 144, 170–71

Consciousness: as c. of action, 6, 10;
class c., 139, 166; and contingence,
10; social c., 11, 139, 166

Conservative, liberal, radical: 84, 111,
145, 169, 172

Consubstantiality: of divine persons,
34, 52, 55; of human beings, 52;
imitative c., 65; real c., 65
Contingence: and empirical existence 10, 76; and impure reality, 78;
matter, c., and intelligible truth, 10;
and potency, 52; as ultimate basis of
there being anything to be conscious
of, 10; as ultimate empirical in order
of consciousness, 10; unintelligible
in itself, 77
Control: and Christ, 29; and free will,
6, 48, 70; higher c., 15, 17, 18, 19,
20, 21, 28; immanent c. of intellect and will not an initiation but a
power of approval or inhibition, 6;
and liberalism, 5 & n. 2, 23, 33; and
philosophy, 11, 33; and thought, 49
Conversion: and multiple dialectic
with grace, 152
Cortés, Donoso, 61 & n. 35, 175 &
n. 75
Creation: end of, and Christ, 61; and
manifestation of Word, 34, 73; new
c., 27, 29, 62; role of Christ in c., 54
Cromwell, Thomas, 66 & n. 5
Crowe, Frederick, 38 n. 1, 44 n. 14,
46 n. 16, 50 n. 21, 105 n. 15, 154 n.
1, 156 nn. 5–6, 171 nn. 26 and 28,
174 n. 33
Culture: and civilization, 149 n. 22;
corruption of, 24; development of,
69; higher c., 24, 101, 138, 139, 149;
humanistic c., 167; and leisure, 36,
45, 58, 101, 138, 139; and lies, 145
& n. 18; and major decline, 171;
and migration, 151; primitive and
higher, 12; and sacrifice, 149, 175
Cupidity, 142, 148, 174
Cynics, 17
Cyprian, 47
Cyreniacs, 17

Dark age: and philosophy, 11; and
rebirth, 146; and subsequent cultural
expansion, 17
Dawson, Christopher, 11 & n. 10, 14 &
n. 12, 18 & n. 14, 101 & n. 11, 129
& n. 4, 151 n. 23, 156
Death: and democracy, 13; and reign
of sin, 121; transmutation of d. by
Christ, 55, 121
Decision(s): and formal object of
analytic concept of history, 132;
and modern states, 23; solidarity of
human d., 98–99
Decline: and animalization of man,
169, 175; in church, 125; compound
d., 111, 115, 142, 144–46, 172; as
consequence of violation of natural
law, 111; goal of d., 140–41, 168–69;
major d., 111, 113–15, 142, 143–44,
169, 170–71; major and minor d.
accelerate each other, 115–16, 145;
major d. proceeds from deformation
of conscience to dethronement of
reason, 143–44; minor d., 111–13,
124, 142–43, 169–70; nature of, 140–
41, 168–69; and penance, charity,
faith, etc., 119, 148; and philosophy,
150; and poverty, chastity, obedience,
120, 148; resistance to major d., 151;
and schism and heresy, 125; and sin,
111, 117, 146, 149, 152, 169, 170,
172, 174; as systematic deviation
from ideal line of history, 140–41,
168; terminal phenomena of d., 116;
three elements in course of major d.,
114. *See also* New order; Progress-
decline-renaissance/redemption
Deduction: of ideal line of history,
138–40; and induction, 137–38,
165–66, 167
Democracy: and death, 13; and
philosophy, 13, 19

Despoiling the Egyptians, 55

Determination: d. of ideal line, 137, 139, 164; historical d. of intellect, 43–46; material and historical d. of will, 43. *See also* Predetermination

Development: Catholic d., 33; of Christian spirituality, 126; cultural d., 101, 152, 167; of dogma, 24, 56 & n. 27, 69, 126; form of intellectual d., 107–10; of human thought, 82–84; line of d. of human mind, 69–70, 137–38; of objective *Geist*, 49, 56, 69; and periods of history, 33; of personality, 100; priority of economic d., 102, 149, 175; and sin, 70–71; of socially minded man, 140; of works of charity and apostolate, 126

Dialectic(s): absolute d., 24, 33; of absolute *Geist*, 69; analysis of, 104, 135–36; d. based on sin, 25; d. defined, 135; d. of evil, 35; d. of fact, 20, 21, 22, 24, 27, 30, 33, 35, 45–46, 69; 'the d.' [d. of history], 25, 103, 104, 132–34, 135, 159–62; d. of major decline, 148; d. of sin, 46, 60, 63, 69, 70, 74, 82, 85–87, 88, 89, 90; d. of thought, 20, 25, 30, 32, 33, 36, 46–47; division of, 134–35; existence of, 133–34, 160–61; as experiment, 103, 132, 160; form of, 133, 161; interaction of d., 103, 134, 161, 169; multiple d., 96, 103, 104, 116, 134, 149, 174; multiple d. with grace, 152, 176–77; multiple d. without grace, 149–551, 176; natural d., 82–85, 86–87, 89, 90–91, 92, 93; in Plato, 14–15, 16; pure d. of fact, 20; rates of, 133, 162; seven d., 33; single d., 134, 149, 174; single d. with grace, 151–52, 175; single d. without grace, 149,

174–75; supernatural component of d., 26–31; supernatural d., 82, 87–88, 89, 90, 94; three categories of d., 104; three periods in dialectics of sin and thought, 33; threefold d. in historic progress of intellect, 45; transferences of multiple d., 112

Differential(s): and bureaucracy, 13; first, second, and third d. of human operation, 44; and flow of activity, 8–9, 32; integrating the d., 8–9, 13, 32

Differentiation(s): d. by *esse absolutum*, 78; d. by *esse relativum*, 78; d. of objective *Geist*, 53; empirical d., 77; geographical d., 101, 160; intelligible d., 77, 89

Disorder: like complex number, 112; and minor decline, 115, 145, 150, 172; objective d., 70, 112, 120, 143, 170

Dogma: and absolute *Geist*, 55–59 & n. 27; development of d., *see* Development: of d.; and human unity, 57; and philosophy, 55; Scholastic systematization of, 30

Earthly task of man, 106, 136, 139, 164

Economic development: priority of, 102, 149, 175; and social dependence, 102; and social unit's enlargement, 101, 102, 149

Economics: and human unity, 72; liberal e. and self-interest, 113, 172; and major decline, 172; and progress-decline, 115; and state, 24, 32

Egoism: and disorder, 120; and enlightened self-interest, 142, 170; individual and group e., 111, 142–43; and minor decline, 119, 148, 174